ONE WEEK LOAN

THE GOOD
SHOPPING GUIDE

Published by the Ethical Marketing Group

First published 2002 by The Ethical Marketing Group
240 Portobello Road, London W11 1LL, UK.
www.thegoodshoppingguide.co.uk.
© Ethical Marketing Ltd, 2002

Publishing Director William Sankey 0044 (0) 207 229 1894
Director of advertising, marketing, logo licensing – Kat Alexander 0044 (0) 207 229 2115
Designed by Deborah Barrow & Gary White
Book produced by Loudmouth Publishing Ltd, Unit 10, 25 Gwydir St, Cambridge, UK
Project manager Charlotte Mulvey, editorial Catherine Hurley, copywriting Richard Synge
Photography by 86 Ltd and First-Rung.com
Media consultancy & public relations by 86 Ltd (see 86.co.uk – 0044 (0) 207 229 1958)

ISBN 0954 2529 0 X

Printed and bound in Great Britain by Cambrian Printers Ltd
on Nordic Swan accredited Festival Superart 115 gsm paper
Distributed by Central Books (orders@centralbooks.com; 0044 (0) 845 458 9911)
Sales enquiries to Troika (troika@sellbooks.demon.co.uk; 00 44 (0) 207 619 0800)

The publishers are grateful to the following for permission to reproduce the photographs on p. 8 Jennifer Bates,
p.196 Calliste Lelliot - Friends of the Earth; p. 122 Nakimera plucking tea, Mpanga, Uganda - Cafédirect;
Thanks also to Craig Morrison, Sam Szanto, Elliot Ronald, Shirin Kiral, Clare Sleeman, Annabel Wetton and Niamh Friel at 86
for their excellent media consultancy. And at ECRA, to Rob Harrison, Bruce Bingham, Sarah Irving, Jonathan Atkinson,
Hannah Berry, Scott Clouder, Matt Fawcett, Mary Rayner, Ruth Rosselson, Jane Turner, Lauren Weadick
Thanks to Yo Fung and EIRIS for help with the ethical investment section. And to Kate Wills and the Day Chocolate Company
for additional PR expertise.

Legal Disclaimer
The Good Shopping Guide aims to provide an independent and authoritative list of mainstream brands and companies
according to research data previously published by and licensed from The Ethical Consumer Research Association. While every
reasonable care is taken to ensure the accuracy of the information in *The Good Shopping Guide*, neither the publisher, the
printers, nor any distributor is responsible for errors or omissions. All data is accepted by us in good faith as being correct at
the time of going to press. Pictures and advertisements are vetted to ensure there is no conflict with this editorial policy. For
further information on the editorial content, fully referenced source materials are available from ECRA on request.

Contents

Foreword by the Ethical Marketing Group

'YOUR TILL RECEIPT IS AS IMPORTANT AS YOUR VOTE'

The Good Shopping Guide is the world's first comprehensive ethical reference guide to clearly list the behaviour of the companies behind everyday consumer brands.

Our objective is to encourage a universally responsible corporate attitude to animal welfare, human rights and the environment.

Companies depend entirely on their customers' goodwill, so we believe that the key to a progressive 21st century lies in the persuasive power of intelligent consumer action.

The Good Shopping Guide informs you of the facts and provides some overall recommendations to help you channel your spending power.

Thank you for all the support from Friends of the Earth, Cafédirect, the Day Chocolate Company, Christian Aid, the World Development Movement, Jupiter, the Forest Stewardship Council, the Ethical Investment Research Service, the Ecology Building Society, Unit(e), Trees for London, Viridian, Wilkinet, Goodness Direct, Organico, Ergo Magazine, Ethical Consumer Magazine, the Environmental Transport Association, RSPB Energy and Survival International.

And thank you especially to the Ethical Consumer Research Association, who have pioneered this field since 1989. This book would not have been possible without their substantial expertise.

WELCOME TO THE GOOD SHOPPING GUIDE

Even in these days of global brands, identical-looking high streets and multinational dominance, consumer power, once mobilised, can still be a powerful force. This book contains all the information you'll need to make even small shopping choices have a big impact.

The Good Shopping Guide aims to help you make informed decisions about what consumer brands are best for the planet, best for animals and best for people everywhere. We hope to make a difference for the environment, for animals and we also want to improve the living standards of poor people in other countries.

Everybody can make a contribution to a better world by the simple choices we make while out shopping. By choosing to buy one kind of coffee over another we can help the farmers who grow it. And most of us know that when we buy an eco-washing-up liquid we help to reduce pollution. But who on earth knows which freezer to buy; what TV manufacturer is the most ethical; what brand of yoghurt is kindest to animals; which consumer goods companies are involved in the arms trade; and which Health and Beauty products are good? *The Good Shopping Guide* tells all – in detail.

SMART CHOICES CAN AND DO HAVE A DIRECT EFFECT ON GLOBAL ISSUES

We don't have to feel powerless about the world's problems. Our till receipts are like voting slips – they can easily be used constructively. This is something that the big corporations will have to notice tomorrow even if their management seems to be unaware and uninformed today.

If you care about things like global warming, pollution, animal testing, factory farming, the arms trade and exploitation of people, you are certainly not alone. You don't have to be a political activist or even to join a campaign. If you care at all, it's really simple to do something about these difficult issues, just by making good choices while you're out shopping.

SMALL DECISIONS – BIG EFFECTS

Our choices can support progressive companies that want to improve the way business is done. And our shopping habits can force changes in the way in which even the largest food corporations and supermarkets do their day-to-day business. It's already happening, with supermarkets displaying fair trade, GM-free and organic foods on their shelves because they know that more and more customers want and appreciate these things.

'Buying ethical products sends support directly to progressive companies working to improve the status quo, while at the same time depriving others that abuse for profit. For example, when you buy an eco-washing-up liquid you're giving its manufacturer the funds it needs to invest in clean technology and advertise its products to a wider market. At the same time, you're no longer buying your old liquid, so its manufacturer loses business and will perhaps change its ways.'

www.ethicalconsumer.org

You can make a difference in lots of ways. You can begin by looking for independent stores in your neighbourhood – it saves on petrol and supports your local community. You can look for fair trade, organic and GM-free foods. And you can choose to buy sustainably-produced or recycled products. Buying eco-cleaning fluids or washing-up liquids gives progressive manufacturers more funds to invest in clean technology and helps to persuade the other manufacturers to think of changing their ways.

Each decision like this has an impact – small in itself but huge when you know that millions of others are doing the same. This book shows that you can be part of the solution, making the world a cleaner and fairer place, rather than part of the problem.

All the information you need to make good and ethical shopping decisions is contained within this book.

WHAT IS GOOD SHOPPING?

Good Shopping is Ethical Shopping, and that means buying things that are made ethically and by companies that act ethically – or in other words without causing harm to or exploiting humans, animals or the environment.

Ethical shopping encourages innovative products and companies and discourages others that prefer to ignore the social and environmental consequences of their practices. It also empowers you, the consumer, and gives you a say in how the products you buy are made and how the manufacturers conduct their business.

Our choices can be both positive, by buying products that you know to be ethical, and negative, by refusing to buy products that you disapprove of.

Ethical shopping can also mean supporting actions like the Nestlé boycott, which targeted all the brands and company subsidiaries to try to force the company to change its marketing of formula baby milk in the Third World.

And you can follow what the Ethical Consumer Research Association (ECRA) calls the 'fully screened approach'. This means looking at all the companies and products together and evaluating which brand is the most ethical. This is the information that *The Good Shopping Guide* brings together in the following pages.

ECRA is part of an ever-growing network of organisations committed to making the world a better place: organisations like Oxfam, Fairtrade Foundation, Traidcraft, Friends of the Earth, Naturewatch, the Soil Association, the Vegetarian Society and the Forest Stewardship Council.

By using this book you will discover more than you ever knew about what goes into the goods you buy or are thinking of buying. You will have the information you need to make clear decisions, either to buy the products of progressive and green companies or to boycott those of unethical companies.

Rob Harrison of ECRA has seen the trend towards ethical shopping grow: 'For the last 30 years or so, multinationals have been trying to shape the decisions of elected governments to fit their vision of a global free market but the ordinary people who buy their products haven't been so convinced. But the scale of opposition from a new wave of ethical consumers has taken companies aback.'

How to use this book

The Good Shopping Guide takes you through all the ethical factors you may want to consider when you are buying products for the home, health and beauty, kitchens, food and drink or financial services.

For each type of product, you will find:

- A summary table – to gain a quick overview on which brands are from the most ethical companies

- A long table – to study the detail across fourteen ethical criteria, to decide precisely which brands are for you

THE BOOK

The Guide gives you the essential environmental, animal welfare and human rights background on a wide range of products, the changes that are being made by the manufacturers and the names of the most progressive companies. It summarises the most important ethical details about the different brands that are available in the UK.

Clear ratings are given for the different brands, covering the companies' environmental reporting, pollution, animal testing, factory farming, workers' rights, involvement in armaments and genetic engineering and other ethical factors.

After a close reading and considering all the companies and products together, you will have all the information you need to make some really switched-on shopping decisions.

When you are in the shops, look out for *The Good Shopping Guide* logo – the badge of authority that says a brand has scored well in our ethicality test. *The Good Shopping Guide* logo will begin to appear in the shops in 2003. You can do your bit by asking for ethical products to be well displayed.

"Of course I'm worried about climate change, but what can I do?"

If you're worried about climate change, you're certainly not alone.

There are millions of us around the world, and together we can make a powerful difference.

- We can make the world's governments turn their promises into action.

- We can campaign for serious investments in wind, wave and solar power.

- We can persuade the UK Government to reject the dangerous policy of expanding nuclear power.

Join us today, and be part of the solution.

To join, call us now on 0800 581 051

To find out more or to join online, visit our website www.foe.co.uk

Friends of the Earth

Friends of the Earth inspires solutions to environmental problems, which make life better for people exist for all the standard toxicity and irritancy tests. But the process of 'validating' these alternative methods has been obstructed, according to BUAV, by industry and regulatory bodies' reluctance to accept these new methods.

Companies need to do two things in order to behave responsibly:

- Invest heavily in developing alternative, non-animal tests and lobby to get them validated
- Postpone the search for new ingredients and use the 8,000 established ingredients until non-animal alternatives to all animal tests have been validated

A full red circle (●) indicates that the company conducts or commissions tests on animals for non-medical products or ingredients *or* sells animal-tested cosmetics, toiletries or household products. An empty red circle (O) indicates that the company conducts or commissions tests on animals for medical products or sells medical products.

2. FACTORY FARMING

A full red circle (●) indicates that the company is: a factory farmer of meat, poultry (broiler and eggs), fish or fur *or* manufactures or supplies intensive farming equipment such as battery cages, beak trimmers, pig crates *or* sells or processes meat, poultry (broiler and eggs), or fur that is not labelled as free range or organic. An empty red circle (O) represents a lessser degree of involvement relative to the other companies on the table.

The definition for this column means that farmers, food manufacturers (such as Heinz) and retailers (such as Asda) of any

meat, eggs and fish will get a lower rating. Animal breeders or 'stock suppliers' and suppliers of equipment such as battery cages, veal crates, etc are bottom rated also, along with those in the fur industry. This column specifically excludes free-range farmers/companies/products, which are dealt with in Other Animal Rights. Dairy farmers and processors are excluded from this column because otherwise all but vegan or organic food producers would be bottom rated, and would produce a column of little practical use to consumers wishing to make a distinction.

3. OTHER ANIMAL RIGHTS

Philosophically speaking, there are two main types of animal campaign group – those that promote concern for animal welfare and those that believe that animals should have 'rights'. The most important 'right' is the right to live – and this category primarily helps animal rights campaigners to identify companies which are involved in the slaughter of animals or the use of animal by-products.

A full red circle (●) indicates that the company is

- a farmer of non-intensive/free range meat, poultry (broilers and eggs) or fish, or is a dairy farmer, or
- a slaughterhouse owner or user of slaughterhouse by-products such as leather and gelatin

An empty red circle (O) represents:

- supply of animal feedstuffs
- sale or processing of free range meat, poultry (broilers and eggs) or fish
- other activities involving the exploitation of animals, e.g. zoos, circuses

The People columns

1. Oppressive regimes

Holding corporations accountable for their presence in oppressive regimes began in earnest during the campaign against South Africa's apartheid system and it has since evolved so that a 'list' of countries, as detailed below, exists. The ranking system for oppression is based on a range of indicators like use of torture, political prisoners, denial of religious freedoms and extrajudicial killings.

This list and, indeed, this column in the table is controversial, partly because many deeply unpopular governments do not appear on the list, but also because some people argue that trade is a way of engaging with and educating oppressive governments.

Companies are rated according to a point system, so middle rated for scoring up to five points, and bottom rated for six points or more under the following system:

Operations by the company or company group or related company in any of the following regimes score TWO points per country: Algeria, Burma, China, Colombia, Indonesia, Iraq, Libya, North Korea, Syria and Yugoslavia.

Operations by the company or company group or related company in any of the following score ONE point per country: Afghanistan, Bahrain, Belorus, Bosnia, Brazil, Cambodia, Croatia, Cuba, Dominican Republic, Egypt, El Salvador, Guatemala, Iran, Kenya, Kuwait, Liberia, Mexico, Nigeria, Pakistan, Peru, the Philippines, Qatar, Russia, Saudi Arabia, Sri Lanka, Sudan, Tajikistan, Tunisia, Turkey and Venezuela.

A company will not score points if all its products sourced from these regimes are marketed as fair trade.

2. Workers' rights

A full red circle (●) or empty red circle (○) represents criticism of the company or its suppliers for infringement of workers' rights, which includes: intimidation of workers by management; use of forced or slave labour; payment of wages below a level which is adequate to live on; a working week of over 48 hours; forced and/or excessive overtime; exploitative use of child labour; denial of the right to associate, form unions or bargain collectively; discrimination on the grounds of race, sex, sexuality, or creed; the provision of inadequate or dangerous working conditions.

3. Irresponsible marketing

All consumers in free-market economies learn to accept that the language of marketing accentuates the positive and plays down the negative. The point at which this becomes 'irresponsible' is difficult to define. ECRA has chosen a fairly strict definition for this category, and we only focus on practices that have direct health implications. Certain activities do avoid this definition. Coca Cola, for example, whose cans manage to find their way to the most impoverished rural settlements in the Third World, and which delivers precious little in the way of nutrition, is often criticised by development analysts. Coke, however, is not marketed as healthy or nutritious. It is simply portrayed as 'fun' so would not be bottom rated.

Four industries generate the bulk of the criticisms for this category: baby milk formula, pharmaceuticals, tobacco and pesticides.

A full red circle (●) indicates marketing of products in a way that has been criticised for causing severe physical harm.

On the tables, an empty red circle (○) indicates the marketing of products in a way that has been criticised as being detrimental to health. (See ECRA Research Supplements for more details).

4. ARMAMENTS

In the table, a full red circle (●) represents involvement in the manufacture or supply of nuclear or conventional weapons including: ships, tanks, armoured vehicles and aircraft; weapons systems components; systems aiding the launch, guidance, delivery or deployment of missiles; fuel; computing; communications services. (See ECRA Research Supplements for detail).

An empty red circle (○) represents the manufacture or supply of non-strategic parts of the military, not including food and drink.

THE EXTRAS COLUMNS

1. GENETIC ENGINEERING

A full red circle (●) represents involvement in:
— the non-medical genetic modification of plants or animals, and/or
— gene-patenting, and/or
— xenotransplantation
An empty red circle (○) represents:
— the manufacture or sale of non-medical products involving or containing

genetically modified organisms (GMOs), and/or
— the manufacture or sale of non-medical products likely to contain GMOs and the lack of clear company group-wide GMO free policy and/or
— public statements in favour of the use of GMOs in non-medical products.
— the development or marketing of medical procedures or products involving genetic modification, which have been criticised on ethical grounds.

2. BOYCOTT CALL

This column can be problematic since a boycott may be called from groups from across the political spectrum. It is important, therefore, to be clear about the reasons why a particular boycott has been called and these are explained in the relevant ECRA Research Supplements.

Some types of campaign group have problems with boycotts. For example, development charities such as CAFOD and Oxfam have contended that boycotts of companies involved in workers' rights abuses could put workers' livelihoods at risk. However, boycotts can be a useful means of exerting economic pressure for change and cannot, therefore, be ignored.

On the table, a full red circle (●) indicates that a boycott of the brand name featured has been called somewhere in the world, or a boycott of the entire company group has been called.

A full amber circle (●) indicates that a boycott of one of the parent company's subsidiaries or other brands has been called somewhere in the world. For more information on specific ongoing UK boycotts, see *www.ethicalconsumer.org*

3. POLITICAL DONATIONS

The political donations column differs from most of the other table columns in that instead of rating companies with a mark for their involvement, we simply inform the reader where donations have been spent. We normally represent this on the table as LAB (Labour), LIB (Liberal) and CON (Conservative). Other symbols on the table have included 'CPS' referring to the Centre for Policy Studies, a Conservative think-tank, and 'BUI' another Conservative Party fund-raising mechanism. Abbreviations such as 'USA' appear where donations have been made in other countries.

We include this column because we do not believe that corporations should fund political parties. There is considerable evidence that the huge wealth of corporations can distort the political process. Elections in the USA particularly can appear to be 'bought' by the candidate with the biggest budgets, and parties with agendas critical of business can be quickly marginalised. In some countries, such as Germany, corporate funding is quite sensibly prohibited by law. Until that occurs in the UK, consumers who agree with this position can use our tables to withdraw their custom from political donors.

4. CODE OF CONDUCT

A full red circle (●) indicates that the parent company has no Code of Conduct for workers' rights at its supplier companies or did not reply to our request for a copy of one.

An empty red circle (○) indicates that the parent company has demonstrated to ECRA or other campaign groups a Code of Conduct for protection of workers' rights.

A green circle (●) indicates that the parent company has demonstrated to ECRA or other campaign groups a Code of Conduct for workers' rights AND effective procedures for independent monitoring of that code or that its products are labelled and certified as fair trade.

VERY PROGRESSIVE BRANDS

In two cases we have promoted a brand up a level in the short tables. This is where the brand is very ethical and progressive (Co-operative Bank and Ecover).

PREVIOUSLY PUBLISHED REPORTS

All the long tables in this book have been previously been published by ECRA in *Ethical Consumer* magazine and /or on Corporate Critic database. ECRA has permitted *The Good Shopping Guide* to reproduce them under licence. ECRA re-checked company ratings in the Guide in May 2002 using the Corporate Critic database (see About ECRA), but please be aware that ratings or ownership of brands may have changed since then. The text of the Buyers' Guides has not been re-written by ECRA since the original publication date (see below for details), and ECRA has given *The Good Shopping Guide* a free hand to edit and re-write the text of each report.

Fully referenced abstracts detailing exactly why each mark was awarded, appear in numbered Research Supplements (see below) and/or on the Corporate Critic database itself. For more information about specific ratings contact ECRA (see page 246)

Key to The Good Shopping Guide Audit Tables

The tables are intended to show at-a-glance which companies own which brands and what sort of activities they are involved in. They also allow people to identify those issues of most concern to them and to ignore issues of no interest.

Within the broad areas of the environment, animals and people we have a number of categories into which we place criticisms of companies. Most are self explanatory, but you can find out more about the definitions and rating system at the Ethical Consumer website (www.ethicalconsumer.org) or by obtaining 'An Introduction to Ethical Consumer' free of charge from ECRA's office.

Brand names

Within the long tables we attempt to profile the brands which together hold the majority of the market share. However, due to space limitations, short buyers' guides usually have a maximum of around 12 brands, while longer buyers' guides are limited to around 25.

Company Group

In this column we list the ultimate holding company (UHC) i.e. the top level of corporate ownership, which may often differ from the brand owner. For instance, the Umbro brand name is owned by Umbro Europe Ltd, but Umbro Europe is owned by venture capital company Doughty Hanson, which is therefore the UHC and appears in this column. It is important to note that the marks on the table represent those of the company group as a whole, so where Umbro is listed on the table the marks refer not just to Umbro but to Doughty Hanson and all companies owned by Doughty Hanson.

Definition of 'related company'

We use the expression 'related company' throughout the book and particularly on the tables. We use this term when there is a formal relationship (usually a small share holding) but not enough to be treated as a direct subsidiary or associate company.

Original publication dates & issue Numbers

Baby Food 63 (Feb/Mar 2000)
Bananas 61 (Oct/Nov 1999)
Banks & Building Socs 72 (Aug/Sept n 2001)
Batteries 46 (Apr/May 1997)
Beer, lager, cider 72 (Feb/Mar 2002)
Biscuits 77 (June/July 2002)
Bread 56 (Dec/Jan 1998-99)
Bottled Water 72 (Feb/Mar 2002)
Butter & Marg 62 (Dec 1999/Jan 2000)

Cat & Dog food 66 (Aug/Sept 2000)
Cereal 63 (Feb/Mar 2000)
Chocolate 60 (Aug/Sept 1999)
Cold Remedies 49 (Oct/Nov 1997))
Computers 65 (June/July 2000)
Cooking Oil 67 (Nov 2000)
Credit Cards 68 (Dec 2000/Jan2001)
Crisps & Snacks 59 (June/July 1999)

Essential Oils 51 (Feb/Mar 1998)
Eye Care 42 (July/Aug 1996)

Fax Machines 55 (Oct/Nov 1998)
Fridges 69 (Feb/Mar 2001)

Household Cleaners 54 (Aug/Sept 1998)

Insurance 63 (Feb/Mar 2000)
Jams & Spreads 68 (Dec 2000/Jan2001)

Kitchen Appliances 62 (Dec 1999/Jan 2000)
Laundry Detergents 57 (Feb/Mar 1999)
Mortgages 70 (Apr/May 2001)

Nappies 57 (Feb/Mar 1999)

Painkillers 55 (Oct/Nov 1998)
Pasta 64 (April/May 2000)
Perfumes & Aftershaves 47 (June/July 1997)

Sanitary Protection 71 (June/July 2001)
Shampoo 74 (Dec 2001/Jan 2002)
Soap 61 (Oct/Nov 1999)
Soft Drinks 65 (June/July 2000)
Soup 66 (Aug/Sept 2000)
Sports Shoes 62 (Dec 1999/Jan 2000)
Sugar 62 (Dec 1999/Jan 2000)
Suntan 65 (June/July 2000)
Supermarkets 71 (June/July 2001)

Tea & Coffee 73 (Oct/Nov2001)
Toothpaste 69 (Feb/March 2001)
Toys 55 (Oct/Nov 1998)
TV & Video 56 (Dec 1998/Jan1999)

Vacuum Cleaners 59 (June/July 1999)
Vitamins 64 (April/May 2000)

Washing Machines 66 (Aug/Sept 2000)
Washing up Liquid 63 (Feb/Mar 2000)
Whisky 49 (Oct/Nov 1997)

Yoghurt 54 (Aug/Sept 1998)

Contact ECRA for a full index of previous reports.

Ethical shopping success

Over the years, and especially since the 1980s, consumers have been making an ever-increasing impact on the way governments and companies behave in all parts of the world. These are just a few examples:

- The campaign against testing cosmetics on animals changed the behaviour of nearly all the main cosmetics companies.

- A boycott in the US against Heinz forced the company to stop catching tuna with purse-seine fishing nets, which used to kill tens of thousands of dolphins each year – the tuna trade and the Whale and Tuna Conservation Society then launched a 'dolphin friendly' logo.

- In 1991, Friends of the Earth launched a campaign against the stocking of tropical timber from unsustainable sources by the six largest DIY chains – the campaign eventually became a consumer boycott and proved very successful. By 1994, all six had agreed to stop selling mahogany.

- There has been such huge growth in the spread of fair-traded goods that supermarkets such as Sainsbury's now advertise them openly.

- Probably the most dramatic single environmental boycott was Greenpeace's campaign in 1995 against the dumping of Shell's oil platform Brent Spar – sales of Shell petrol were down by 70 per cent in some German outlets and the company gave in after only a few days.

- Increasing numbers of clothing retail companies and sports shoes manufacturers have adopted codes of conduct about the conditions of the workers making their goods.

- Ethical consumerism encouraged the phasing out of the worst ozone-depleting and greenhouse gases used in fridges and freezers – in 1994, Electrolux followed manufacturers Bosch, Siemens, Liebherr and AEG in replacing ozone damaging HCFCs and HFCs with hydrocarbons.

- The UK campaign against genetically modified (GM) foods was so successful that the leading companies changed their policies – eight supermarket chains in the UK now sell their own GM-free own-brands.

- The consumer boycott of fruit and wine and other products from apartheid South Africa helped to free Nelson Mandela and to bring about democratic change.

15 Good shopping principles

1 ONLY BUY BRANDS FROM THE "GOOD SHOPPING" LISTS FEATURED IN THIS BOOK
Don't worry if you have some questionable brands around you today – just gradually try to replace them with Good Shopping brands over the next few years.

2 LOCAL SHOPS
Look out for local, independent stores. Using them means you use your car less. They offer more personal service and they support the local community.

3 HEALTH FOOD SHOPS
These are the best places to support. They tend to stock fair trade, vegetarian and organic products as well as vitamins and herbal remedies.

4 FAIR TRADE
Look out for Fairtrade Foundation marked products, which guarantee that workers have been fairly rewarded for their labour. Organisations like Oxfam (01865 311311) and Traidcraft (0191 491 1001) also sell fair trade goods on the high street or via mail order catalogues.

5 PRODUCTS NOT TESTED ON ANIMALS
Look for 'not tested on animals' labels or contact BUAV (020 7700 4888) or Naturewatch (01242 252871) for an approved product guide.

6 VEGETARIAN AND VEGAN PRODUCTS
Look out for the Vegetarian Society symbol. It is hard to completely avoid animal products but the Vegan Society publishes the Animal Free Shopper.

7 ORGANIC PRODUCE
Organic food is free of chemical fertilisers and pesticides. Look out for the Soil Association symbol or you can contact the association (0117 929 0661) to find your nearest outlet.

8 NON-GM FOOD
Although 70% of the public oppose the use of genetically modified food, it is increasingly finding its way into our diet. Look out for GM-free labels, the Vegetarian Society symbol or the Soil Association symbols. These all guarantee GM-free.

9 ETHICAL MONEY
Choose an ethical investment fund as well as one of the more ethical banks and mortgages. These decisions are key as they involve so much money.

10 RECYCLING AND SECOND-HAND GOODS
Recycled and second-hand products save resources and reduce pressure on landfill sites. Many everyday things, and especially paper, printer cartridges and TVs, can be 'recycled'. For advice on recycling points in your area contact Wasteline (0870 243 0136).

11 WOOD PRODUCTS
Many timber products have originated from virgin rainforests or unsustainably managed forests. The Forest Stewardship Council (01686 413916) operates independent verification of sustainable timber and paper products. Look out for the FSC logo.

12 GETTING AROUND
Walk as much as you can and use public transport (where it's any good!) When you use a car, try to journey share as much as you can – too many of us drive solo in cars.

13 ENERGY
Choose energy efficient brands where you can – there are several different rating and labelling systems, including one run by the Energy Saving Trust, a non-profit organisation partly run by the government. Also make sure you switch to one of the greener electricity suppliers.

14 SUPPORT THE ADVERTISERS IN THIS BOOK
All our advertisers are ethical brands and have been vetted. We would never accept low scoring brands. So please, support these brands.

15 LOOK OUT FOR THE GOOD SHOPPING GUIDE ETHICAL 2003 LOGO.
If you see this logo you know that brand has scored well on our ethical audit analysis, which is based on the work of The Ethical Consumer Research Association, leading independent researchers since 1989. You may see this logo on selected products from January 2003.

Did you know?

- Transport pollution is the largest single cause of global warming, and the average item you buy in a supermarket has travelled 1,000 miles – and that's before you buy it!
- If everyone in the UK bought one jar of fair trade coffee a month, 2.5 million people (the farmers and their families) would benefit.
- The fair trade product range now includes coffee, drinking chocolate, chocolate bars, orange juice, tea, honey, sugar and bananas.
- Chlorine pollution is a huge threat to the ozone layer. Detergents transfer their chlorine into the air. Chlorine is used in bleach, mould removers and many toilet cleaners. There are ecological alternatives.
- Around the world, over 31 million personal computers are thrown away every year. For every three computers now built, two become obsolete.
- It's estimated that there are 20 million potentially toxic redundant mobile phones in the UK.
- A VCR on standby uses almost as much electric current as one playing a tape. Every year in the UK, VCRs use £113 million and TVs £50 million worth of electricity just waiting to be switched on.
- More than 50% of the heat lost from your home is through loft spaces and walls.
- The most efficient kind of heating for your home would be a condensing boiler, which contains an extra heat exchanger. It also saves on cost.
- Disposable nappies pose a major waste management problem and account for 4% of landfill waste in the UK. The average baby gets through 5,840 of them.

'Every purchase you make has either a direct or an indirect effect on the environment. When you exercise your power by choosing where and what to buy, and where and what NOT to buy, you help change the world for the better.'

Go Make a Difference! *The Ecologist*

WORKING CONDITIONS

Maria works at a factory in Haiti making shirts. Despite ten-hour shifts, she earns so little that she still lives in extreme poverty. She cannot feed her children properly, so they fill their bellies with sugar water to help kill their hunger. The factory conditions are terrible. She gets wages deducted if she visits the toilet too often. She is scared to join a union as her friends have lost their jobs for joining.

Wendy, a 15-year-old girl from Honduras, told the US Congress in 1996 that she had been working in a factory sewing trousers since she was 13, along with about another 100 young teenagers. "Sometimes they kept us all night long, working... The supervisors scream at us and yell at us to work faster. Sometimes they throw the garment in your face, or grab and shove you... Sometimes the managers touch the girls. Pretending it's a joke they touch our legs. Many of us would like to go to night school but we can't because they constantly force us to work overtime."

Did you know... about green energy?

It's now possible to buy power from the company that offers the cleanest electricity rather than having to deal with your local company. This means that thousands of householders can choose to pay for their electrical appliances to be powered by companies which are investing in clean renewable energy, instead of coal, gas or nuclear.

Conventional power stations are the single largest source of greenhouse gas emissions in the UK. Green energy helps fight climate change by reducing the production of carbon dioxide. So choosing green electricity is an easy way to help tackle climate change and reduce pollution, and can add as little as £1 a week to the average fuel bill.

There are basically two types of green electricity tariffs:

- Energy-based – where the supplier buys renewable energy to match the amount you use
- Fund-based – where the supplier puts money aside to fund green projects.

Some suppliers use a combination of both.

Since April 2002, a new law requires all electricity suppliers to buy some green power (currently 3%). Welcome as this is, it has made it difficult to assess which companies are leading the way and which are doing the legal minimum.

The Good Shopping Guide recommends you choose from:

- unit(e)
- Ecotricity
- Green Energy UK
- RSPB Energy
  (from Scottish and Southern Energy)
- Green Energy Offer
  (from Scottish Power)

This is a very important decision as here we can directly influence energy policy.

WHO GIVES A DAM

...ABOUT THE ENVIRONMENT?

Global warming is an ongoing problem. However, it is possible for you to do your bit. Electricity generated from renewable sources avoids the greenhouse gases that result from burning fossil fuels.

WE DO!

At Scottish and Southern Energy – the UK's largest generator from renewables – we care about the environment. In partnership with Europe's largest wildlife conservation charity, we have developed a unique **'green energy'** scheme, which directly helps the environment today and for the future...

RSPB Energy

RSPB Energy electricity is produced from renewable sources, including hydro-power and wind power, which do not create harmful emissions. And **RSPB Energy** also raises hundreds of thousands of pounds to help conservation and the environment – used to support new renewable development, and to acquire and manage areas affected by global warming.*

...YOU CAN TOO!

...at **no extra cost**.*
It's hassle-free to switch to **RSPB Energy**.
Same meters and wires – so no disruption to you –
no forms to fill in – **it couldn't be simpler!**

Extra benefit – you could also save money on your gas through **RSPB Energy**.

Phone us **FREE** today on **0800 0288 552** (quoting code GSRV)

or visit our website at **www.rspbenergy.co.uk**

RSPB Energy

helping conservation with
☰ Scottish and Southern Energy

Good Home

COMPANY CONSIDERATIONS

Two-thirds of the UK market is supplied by imports from Europe, with only a few companies such as Hotpoint, Creda and Belling continuing to manufacture in the UK.

The Good Shopping Guide best scores go to Belling, Candy, Hoover, LG and Miele. See the big table overleaf for more details.

- Candy
- Hoover
- LG
- Miele

- Ariston
- Blomberg
- Brandt
- De Dietrich
- Indesit
- Samsung
- Whirlpool

- AEG
- Beko
- Bosch
- Creda
- Hotpoint
- Tricity Bendix
- Zanussi

BRAND NAME	ENVIRONMENT				ANIMALS			PEOPLE				EXTRAS				Company group
	Environmental Reporting	Pollution	Nuclear Power	Other	Animal Testing	Factory Farming	Other Animal Rights	Oppressive Regimes	Workers' Rights	Irresponsible Marketing	Armaments	Genetic Engineering	Boycott Call	Political Donations		
AEG	○	●	◉	●	●	●	●	●	●	●	◉	●	●	USA		Wallenberg
ARISTON	○	●	●	○	●	●	●	●	●	○	●	●	●			Fineldo Spa
BEKO	○	●	●	●	●	●	●	○	●	●	○	●	●			Koc Holding
BLOMBERG	●	●	●	●	●	●	●	○	●	●	○	●	●			ELCO
BOSCH	●	●	●	●	●	●	●	●	○	●	●	●	●			Robert Bosch/Siemens
BRANDT	●	●	●	●	●	●	●	○	●	●	○	●	●			ELCO
CANDY	●	●	●	●	●	●	●	●	●	●	●	●	●			IFEM
CREDA	●	◉	●	●	●	●	●	○	●	●	●	●	●	USA		Merloni/General Electric
DE DIETRICH	●	◉	●	●	●	●	●	○	●	●	○	●	●			ELCO
HOOVER	●	●	●	●	●	●	●	●	●	●	●	●	●			IFEM
HOTPOINT	●	●	●	●	●	●	●	○	●	●	●	●	●	USA		Merloni/General Electric
INDESIT	○	●	●	○	●	●	●	●	●	○	●	●	●			Fineldo Spa
LG	●	●	●	●	●	●	●	●	●	●	●	●	●			LG Electronics
MIELE	●	●	●	●	●	●	●	●	●	●	○	●	●			Miele & Cie
SAMSUNG	●	●	●	○	●	●	●	●	○	●	●	●	●			Samsung
TRICITY BENDIX	○	●	◉	●	●	●	●	●	●	●	◉	●	●	USA		Wallenberg
WHIRLPOOL	●	●	●	●	●	●	●	●	○	●	◉	●	●			Whirlpool
ZANUSSI	○	◉	◉	●	●	●	●	●	●	●	◉	●	●	USA		Wallenberg

Key

- ● Top rating (no criticisms found)
- ○ Middle rating
- ● Bottom rating
- ◉ A related company has a bottom rating and the company itself has a middle rating
- ○ A related company has a middle rating
- ● A related company has a bottom rating

Source: ECRA–See page 14 for full key to symbols.

Fridges & freezers

We can chill with a clean conscience if we bear a few things in mind when we buy a fridge or freezer unit. First and most important, we should look for the most energy-efficient models. Next, we need to be sure that the kind of coolant gas the appliance uses does as little harm to the environment as possible. And we should also ask a few questions about the manufacturing companies and their wider policies.

ENERGY USE

Over the lifetime of each fridge and freezer, we probably spend about twice as much on powering it as we did on buying it. This is why we need to look out for the most energy-efficient machines. A less efficient one may be cheaper to buy, but it will be costing much more to run from the moment we switch it on.

Energy labelling is now compulsory for fridges and freezers. Most brands have models available that are classed as A or B. A-rated models use about half as much energy as C-rated ones. 'Energy plus' ratings are awarded to models – fridge/freezers only so far – that are even more efficient. These use as little as half the electricity of the average appliance currently on sale. The EU also awards 'eco-labels' to energy efficient models that are manufactured with minimal environmental impacts, Vestfrost of Denmark is an example of a company that has received this label.

COOLANTS

When CFC coolant gas went out of production because it was harming the ozone layer, manufacturers switched to HCFCs and then to HFCs (hydrofluorocarbons). There is still widespread use of HFCs in fridges even though they are known to have high global

60-SECOND GREEN GUIDE

- Buy an A-rated hydrocarbon (R600a) appliance (it will be labelled 'CFC- and HFC-free')
- When buying a fridge/freezer consider opting for a two-control model so that one of the units (for example the fridge) can be switched off when you go on holiday
- Chest freezers are more energy efficient than upright models
- Make sure your old appliance is professionally de-gassed and preferably recycled – it will probably contain CFCs or HFCs

warming potential and their production results in toxic waste.

One of the best options to look for is the 'R600a' hydrocarbon coolant (labelled 'CFC- and HFC-free'). This has a lower global warming potential, is non-toxic and is more efficient than HFCs.

DISPOSAL

Old fridges and freezers contain a number of toxic substances, including CFC and HFC coolants and flame-retardant chemicals, so it is crucial that they are disposed of safely and correctly. Some manufacturers and retailers take back old models and may offer trade-ins, so it is worth ringing them first. Otherwise we can call our local council for advice, look in the Yellow Pages under 'Recycling'.

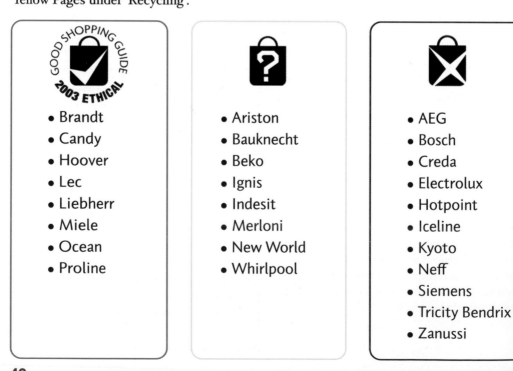

GOOD SHOPPING GUIDE 2003 ETHICAL

- Brandt
- Candy
- Hoover
- Lec
- Liebherr
- Miele
- Ocean
- Proline

- Ariston
- Bauknecht
- Beko
- Ignis
- Indesit
- Merloni
- New World
- Whirlpool

- AEG
- Bosch
- Creda
- Electrolux
- Hotpoint
- Iceline
- Kyoto
- Neff
- Siemens
- Tricity Bendrix
- Zanussi

FRIDGES & FREEZERS

BRAND NAME	ENVIRONMENT	ANIMALS	PEOPLE	EXTRAS	Company group
AEG				USA	Wallenberg Family
ARISTON					Fineldo Spa
BAUKNECHT					Whirlpool Corp
BEKO					Koc Holding
BOSCH					Robert Bosch/Siemens
BRANDT					ELCO
CANDY					IFEM
CREDA				USA	GE/Merloni
ELECTROLUX				USA	Wallenberg Family
HOOVER					IFEM
HOTPOINT				USA	GE/Merloni
ICELINE					The Big Food Group
IGNIS					Whirlpool Corp
INDESIT					Fineldo SpA
KYOTO					The Big Food Group
LEC					Sime Darby Bhd
LIEBHERR					Liebherr International SA
MERLONI					Fineldo Spa
MIELE					Miele & Cie GmbH
NEFF					Robert Bosch/Siemens
NEW WORLD					Fineldo Spa
OCEAN					ELCO
PROLINE				CON	Kingflsher Plc
SIEMENS					Robert Bosch/Siemens
TRICITY BENDIX				USA	Wallenberg Family
WHIRLPOOL					Whirlpool Corp
ZANUSSI				USA	Wallenberg Family

Column headings (left to right):
ENVIRONMENTAL REPORTING, POLLUTION, NUCLEAR POWER, OTHER, ANIMAL TESTING, FACTORY FARMING, OTHER ANIMAL RIGHTS, OPPRESSIVE REGIMES, WORKERS' RIGHTS, IRRESPONSIBLE MARKETING, ARMAMENTS, GENETIC ENGINEERING, BOYCOTT CALL, POLITICAL DONATIONS

Key

- ● Top rating (no criticisms found)
- ○ Middle rating
- ● Bottom rating
- ● A related company has a bottom rating and the company itself has a middle rating
- ○ A related company has a middle rating
- ● A related company has a bottom rating

Source: ECRA-See page 14 for full key to symbols.

41

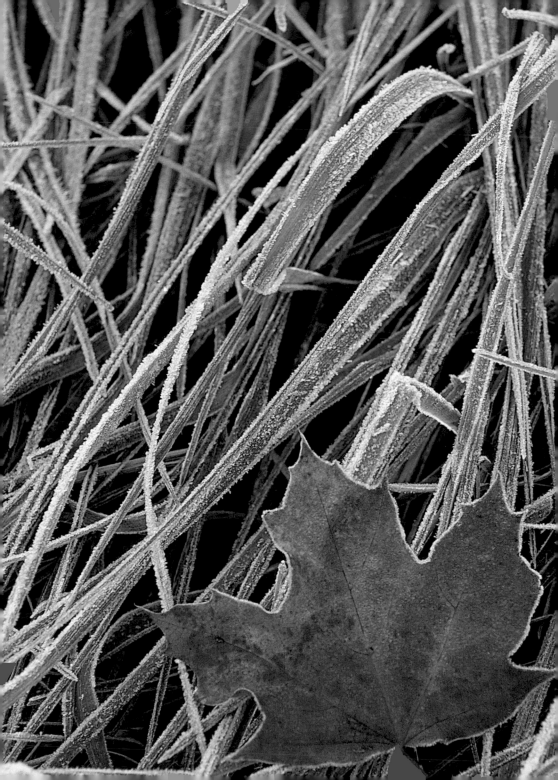

Vacuum cleaners

Beating the dust problem is not just a matter of having a powerful vacuum cleaner but of having one that is both energy-efficient and easy to handle around the home. That's why for some of us a manual carpet sweeper may be all we need. But the bigger the house the more likely it is that we will want quite a large machine with excellent reach and sucking power.

POWER AND NOISE

Vacuum cleaners are rated by manufacturers in terms of their wattage – a measure that only reveals the size of the motor. But as the average vacuum cleaner wastes most of the electricity used in heat and noise, the power rating does not necessarily provide us with any helpful information in deciding upon effectiveness.

Only about a quarter of the power output is actual suction power. Electrolux makes a SmartVac range with 450 W of suction from 1500 W input and this is high compared to most. Miele makes a model called Naturell with an energy-saving 800 W motor. Manufacturers might be willing to disclose the suction power data upon request, but this information is not normally found on the label.

There are plans to encourage producers to make more efficient machines by way of voluntary labelling schemes. One group working on this is the Group for Efficient Appliances, a forum of representatives from national energy agencies and European governments. Most EU member states are represented but at the time of this EC report there was no UK representative – making it seem that there was no enthusiasm for recycling issues in the UK.

BAGS AND DUST

It might be argued that Dyson machines have less of an impact on the environment because they don't use paper and resources to produce vacuum bags, but there is disagreement about whether or not a collection bag interferes with the efficiency of the suction. Dyson asserts that because its machines have no bag their efficiency is constant.

Machines with bags tend to drop in efficiency as the bag fills, and this reduces the amount that is picked up. To counter this, manufacturers such as Miele claim that the bag acts as an extra filter for dust particles and also prolongs the life of the motor.

Certain manufacturers, such as Nilfisk and Medivac, make vacuum cleaners with 'high efficiency filters' to minimise the re-emission of dust. The British Allergy Foundation (BAF) has a system of approval for vacuum cleaners which includes double-blind testing such that the testers have no idea who the individual manufacturers are.

ALTERNATIVES

If buying a vacuum cleaner, it is always possible to buy a reconditioned machine second-hand – or to repair a broken one. Handheld brushes are often more efficient than you might think and simply involve a little elbow grease, although they probably don't pick up the smaller particles which can cause allergic reactions. There are always old-style carpet sweepers, which are manual, non-electric and work a treat.

GOOD SHOPPING GUIDE 2003 ETHICAL

- Dyson
- MediVac
- Nifilsk
- Vax

?

- Hoover
- Miele
- Morphy Richards
- Rowenta

✗

- AEG
- Electrolux
- Hitachi
- Panasonic
- Philips

BRAND NAME	ENVIRONMENT	ANIMALS	PEOPLE	EXTRAS	Company group

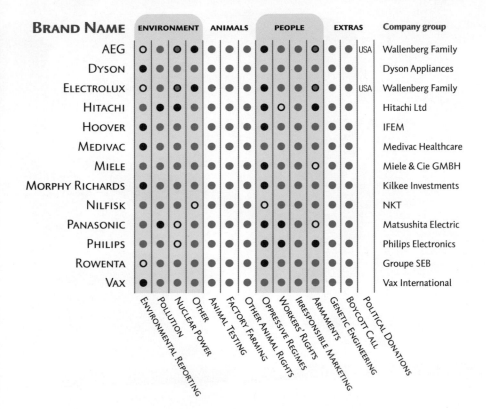

BRAND NAME	Company group
AEG	Wallenberg Family
DYSON	Dyson Appliances
ELECTROLUX	Wallenberg Family
HITACHI	Hitachi Ltd
HOOVER	IFEM
MEDIVAC	Medivac Healthcare
MIELE	Miele & Cie GMBH
MORPHY RICHARDS	Kilkee Investments
NILFISK	NKT
PANASONIC	Matsushita Electric
PHILIPS	Philips Electronics
ROWENTA	Groupe SEB
VAX	Vax International

Column categories (listed diagonally):
ENVIRONMENTAL REPORTING · POLLUTION · NUCLEAR POWER · OTHER · ANIMAL TESTING · FACTORY FARMING · OTHER ANIMAL RIGHTS · OPPRESSIVE REGIMES · WORKERS' RIGHTS · IRRESPONSIBLE MARKETING · ARMAMENTS · GENETIC ENGINEERING · BOYCOTT CALL · POLITICAL DONATIONS

Key

- ● Top rating (no criticisms found)
- ○ Middle rating
- ● Bottom rating
- ◉ A related company has a bottom rating and the company itself has a middle rating
- ○ A related company has a middle rating
- ● A related company has a bottom rating

Source: ECRA-See page 14 for full key to symbols.

Kitchen appliances

Where would we be without our cups of tea or coffee and slices of toast in the morning? As they're our basic start-up fuel it's little wonder that the kitchen appliances we get through most are kettles and toasters. They wear out so fast that we often have to think of buying new ones – a good example of 'built-in obsolescence' at the heart of our lives. That's why the focus of this report is on environmental issues, energy consumption and packaging. As well as kettles and toasters, the report covers other kitchen appliances like blenders, food processors, hand blenders, hand mixers, food mixers, juicers and deep fat fryers.

OUR THROW-AWAY CULTURE

At least six million kitchen appliances are discarded each year, mostly thrown into dustbins, with the result that proper recycling is very unlikely to happen. Friends of the Earth would like to see much higher recycling or re-use targets for waste electrical and electronic equipment; the organisation argues in favour of making products last longer, designing them for easy repair or for easy replacement of worn-out components, as well as for easy recycling for parts that cannot be re-used. FoE says that this should be the responsibility of the manufacturers, so that they carry the costs of recycling or disposal of their products.

Even if a piece of equipment seems to have reached the end of its life, that doesn't mean it's no longer usable. Second-hand shops often take our old equipment and there are schemes around the UK to recover discarded electrical equipment.

Wastewatch recommends that old appliances are not dumped in the bin but taken to a civic amenity site where they can be added to other scrap for recycling. Information is available from the local authority, which will have a recycling officer, or from Wastewatch (*www.wastewatch.org.uk*).

MATERIALS USED

Various materials, such as stainless steel, iron and plastics, are used in most kitchen appliances. All the associated ills of mining and manufacturing come into play – toxic waste, pollution, energy wastage and greenhouse gas emissions. Of course these things are going to exist anyway, but a good way for us to minimise these impacts is to avoid buying new products, choosing second-hand or reconditioned items instead.

TRIMMING DOWN

The new concealed-element kettles are good in that they permit the boiling of only small amounts of water, whereas old-style kettles tend to require excessive amounts of water to work.

Weighing up how often an item will be used can help us decide how necessary it is. If we're unlikely to use it really often do we really need it? It also helps to think about ease of use, as there may be another way to do a job without getting over-complicated gadgets that are often difficult to clean. For example, a blender does many of the same jobs as a food processor but uses smaller amounts of energy.

ENERGY USE

The energy efficiency of electrical appliances varies from model to model.

As there is no eco-labelling scheme for small kitchen appliances, consumers have to rely on product packaging displaying the energy usage. A kettle draws up to 3KW and when millions are turned on at about the same time, the increase in demand is massive. Compared to electricity, gas is 30 per cent more energy-efficient, which is why kettles used on gas cookers are generally a better option than electric kettles.

Hard water leaves a build-up of calcium carbonate, which reduces a kettle's energy efficiency – this can easily be cleaned off from time to time with vinegar.

Hand-operated kitchen appliances, naturally enough, are the most energy-efficient kinds you can buy – not least the whisks, forks and knives that are absolutely essential for cooking with!

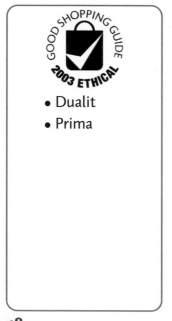

- Dualit
- Prima

- De' Longhi
- Kenwood
- Morphy Richards
- Moulinex
- Pifco
- Rowenta
- Russell Hobbs
- Salton
- Swan
- Tefal

- Braun
- Breville
- Bush
- Goodmans
- Hinari
- Philips

BRAND NAME	ENVIRONMENT				ANIMALS			PEOPLE				EXTRAS			Company group
	Environmental Reporting	Pollution	Nuclear Power	Other	Animal Testing	Factory Farming	Other Animal Rights	Oppressive Regimes	Workers' Rights	Irresponsible Marketing	Armaments	Genetic Engineering	Boycott Call	Political Donations	
BRAUN	●	●	●	○	●	●	●	●	●	●	○	●	●		Gillette
BREVILLE	●	●	●	○	●	●	●	○	●	●	●	●	●		Alba Plc
BUSH	●	●	●	○	●	●	●	○	●	●	●	●	●		Alba Plc
DE'LONGHI	●	●	●	●	●	●	●	○	●	●	●	●	●		De'longhi Spa
DUALIT	●	●	●	●	●	●	●	●	●	●	●	●	●		Dualit Ltd
GOODMANS	●	●	●	○	●	●	●	○	●	●	●	●	●		Alba Plc
HINARI	●	●	●	○	●	●	●	○	●	●	●	●	●		Alba Plc
KENWOOD	●	●	●	●	●	●	●	○	●	●	●	●	●		De'Longhi Spa
MORPHY RICHARDS	●	●	●	●	●	●	●	●	●	●	●	●	●		Kilkee Investments
MOULINEX	○	●	●	●	●	●	●	●	●	●	●	●	●		Groupe SEB
PHILIPS	●	●	○	●	●	●	●	●	●	●	●	●	●		Philips Electronics
PIFCO	●	●	●	●	●	●	●	○	●	●	●	●	●		Salton Inc
PRIMA	●	●	●	●	●	●	●	●	●	●	●	●	●		Prima International Group
ROWENTA	○	●	●	●	●	●	●	●	●	●	●	●	●		Groupe SEB
RUSSELL HOBBS	●	●	●	●	●	●	●	○	●	●	●	●	●		Salton Inc
SALTON	●	●	●	●	●	●	●	○	●	●	●	●	●		Salton Inc
SWAN	○	●	●	●	●	●	●	●	●	●	●	●	●		Groupe SEB
TEFAL	○	●	●	●	●	●	●	●	●	●	●	●	●		Groupe SEB

Key

● Top rating (no criticisms found)

○ Middle rating

● Bottom rating

◉ A related company has a bottom rating and the company itself has a middle rating

○ A related company has a middle rating

● A related company has a bottom rating

Source: ECRA-See page 14 for full key to symbols.

TV & video

If too much TV rots the brain, then we're probably all done for, but at least we can try to watch only what we really like – it's amazing how much electricity that could save, *and* it would prevent the box from wearing out so fast.

DON'T DUMP THAT SET

We dump around 2.5 million TV sets every year in the UK. Landfilled or incinerated sets are a loss of resources and a potential pollution hazard – plastics and cathode ray tubes can contain toxic substances. If we're getting a new set, we should look for a higher quality and more durable model that can be upgraded in future. If we want to get rid of an old one, we should take it to a second-hand or charity shop. If the old one is broken and no one will take it, it's best to take it to the civic amenity site where it can be used for scrap or recycled.

ENERGY EFFICIENCY

According to one scientific estimate, producing the energy necessary to power our TV viewing creates 7 million tonnes of carbon dioxide and 10,000 tonnes of sulphur dioxide per year. Manufacturers seem to have picked up on this and, as a rule, newer TVs and video recorders are more energy-efficient than earlier ones.

Even in standby mode, we waste about £12 million in electricity consumption a year, Friends of the Earth has estimated. A *Which?* study in 1998 found that Sony, Ferguson, Matsui, Samsung and Sharp came out best, using under 5 watts in standby mode – compared with more than 10 watts used by Mitsubishi, Hitachi, Toshiba and Sanyo models.

MATERIALS

A TV set requires a surprisingly large amount of raw materials. Making the glass screen needs sand and electricity, while the glass for the cathode ray tube contains lead oxide and is coated in graphite to absorb X-rays – these impurities make the tube the hardest component to recycle and this is partly why liquid crystal displays (LCDs) are a less environmentally damaging alternative to conventional screens.

The making of circuit boards uses chemicals, water and energy and generates more hazardous waste than any other part of the TV, especially airborne particulate pollution and chemical waste. TVs and video casings often use brominated flame retardants (BFRs), the making of which can have nasty effects on animal and human health. Friends of the Earth has been campaigning for BFRs to be outlawed –

there is more information on the FoE website *(www.foe.co.uk)*.

Damage to viewers

TVs and videos emit non-ionising radiation over a range of frequencies. Although currently no proven adverse health links exist, the issue stimulates contentious debate and it is best to be cautious, by sitting at least six feet away from the screen and, after use, by switching off devices fully, especially in bedrooms.

60-second green guide

- Buy second-hand TVs and videos where possible
- Switch off when you're not watching instead of leaving the TV on standby
- Don't sit too near a TV
- Favour smaller sets and/or check out LCD screens
- If the TV or video breaks, see if it can be repaired, or make sure it is recycled

- Akai
- Bang & Olufsen
- Casio
- Grundig
- LG
- Sanyo

- Bush
- Ferguson
- Goodmans
- Hinari
- Matsui
- Philips
- Samsung
- Sharp
- Thomson

- Aiwa
- Beko
- Hitachi
- JVC
- Mitsubishi
- Panasonic
- Sony
- Toshiba

BRAND NAME	ENVIRONMENT	ANIMALS	PEOPLE	EXTRAS	Company group
AIWA					Sony Corp
AKAI					Prima International Group
BANG & OLUFSEN					Bang & Olufsen
BEKO					Koc Holding
BUSH					Alba Plc
CASIO					Casio Computer CO
FERGUSON					Thomson Multimedia
GOODMANS					Alba Plc
GRUNDIG					Grundig AG
HINARI					Alba Plc
HITACHI					Hitachi Ltd
JVC					Matsushita Electric
LG					LG Electronics
MATSUI				LAB	Dixons Group
MITSUBISHI					Mitsubishi
PANASONIC					Matsushita Electric
PHILIPS					Philips Flectronics
SAMSUNG					Samsung Co Ltd
SANYO					Sanyo Electric Co
SHARP					Sanwa Group
SONY					Sony Corp
THOMSON					Thomson Multimedia
TOSHIBA					Mitsui Group

Column categories (left to right):
ENVIRONMENTAL REPORTING, POLLUTION, NUCLEAR POWER, OTHER, ANIMAL TESTING, FACTORY FARMING, OTHER ANIMAL RIGHTS, OPPRESSIVE REGIMES, WORKERS' RIGHTS, CODE OF CONDUCT, IRRESPONSIBLE MARKETING, ARMAMENTS, GENETIC ENGINEERING, BOYCOTT CALL, POLITICAL DONATIONS

Key

● Top rating (no criticisms found)

O Middle rating

● Bottom rating

◉ A related company has a bottom rating and the company itself has a middle rating

○ A related company has a middle rating

● A related company has a bottom rating

Source: ECRA-See page 14 for full key to symbols.

Switching to renewable electricity is a breeze.

Switch to unit[e] for clean, non polluting electricity and not only will you be showing your support for renewable energy, but you will also be helping to secure the future of wind and small hydro generation in the UK.

Apply online at
www.unit-e.co.uk/gs

unit [e]   Powering a cleaner world
0845 601 1410

Computers

Computers may be revolutionising our lives in all kinds of unexpected ways but they have not turned the world into a cleaner or a less stressful place.

In fact, they have created huge environmental pollution problems. As they become obsolete so quickly, millions are abandoned or junked every week, but the problems start with the manufacturing process. Since the 1980s, the rush to sell the latest computers in high volumes has tempted manufacturers to cut corners both with the materials they use and with working conditions in component factories, which are located all over the world.

We guide you through the key points to be aware of when considering buying a new 'whole system' computer. We also encourage you to consider upgrading your existing machine, or alternatively to buy a reconditioned machine, rather than buying a new one.

FAST TURN-AROUND

Computers become obsolete far quicker than any other kind of electrical equipment. Levels of waste of electrical equipment are increasing at six times that of other domestic and industrial waste, and information technology equipment makes up 39 per cent of the total, compared to televisions and audio equipment with just 8 per cent.

Studies in the US suggest that we have not even begun to deal with the serious problem of computer disposal. It is estimated that over three-quarters of all computers are stockpiled in attics, cellars and office storage cupboards. They are toxic time bombs, containing not only materials such as lead, cadmium, mercury and hexavalent chromium but also some very nasty compounds like brominated flame retardants (BFRs). Landfill sites and incinerators cannot be expected to dispose of such materials safely.

The EU's directive on Waste Electrical and Electronic Equipment has gone some way to making producers of electronic equipment responsible for disposal, with a view to reducing local councils' recycling costs. It is hoped that the directive will also persuade the manufacturers to use materials that are easier to re-use and recycle.

MAKING A MESS

Computers are made up of modular parts, each of which contains many different components, often produced by different manufacturers around the world. Previously, much of the highly skilled work, such as silicon chip manufacture, was undertaken in the US. Semiconductor production uses more toxic gases than any other industry, with dangers for the workforce. Because of protests in the US, the computer manufacturers have been moving their most dangerous and heavily polluting stages of production to Latin America, where wages and environmental standards are lower.

IBM has made some investments in environmental design and was the first to make a computer using 100 per cent recycled plastic in all its major parts. IBM and Hewlett Packard were among the first major companies to ban the use of BFRs (see page 51) in computer casing, although they continued to rely on suppliers of components that still contained such compounds.

UPGRADING AND RECONDITIONING

The most obvious sign of age in a computer is the speed of its main processor, the price of which increases the further up the scale you go. A positive step for the future would be for manufacturers to sell processor upgrades similar to that of software.

It is possible to buy a second-hand branded, out-of-the-box computer, which has been fully reconditioned with a new keyboard, mouse and software, direct from the factory and still under warranty. Second-user PCs can be bought on the internet or by mail order.

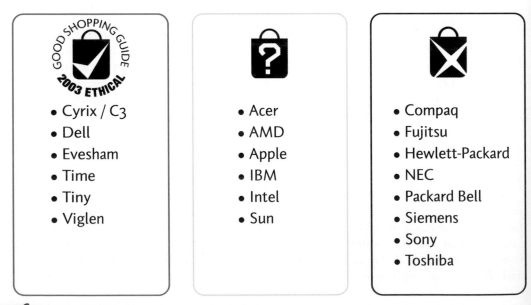

GOOD SHOPPING GUIDE
2003 ETHICAL

- Cyrix / C3
- Dell
- Evesham
- Time
- Tiny
- Viglen

- Acer
- AMD
- Apple
- IBM
- Intel
- Sun

- Compaq
- Fujitsu
- Hewlett-Packard
- NEC
- Packard Bell
- Siemens
- Sony
- Toshiba

Brand Name	ENVIRONMENT				ANIMALS			PEOPLE					EXTRAS			Company group
	Environmental Reporting	Pollution	Nuclear Power	Other	Animal Testing	Factory Farming	Other Animal Rights	Oppressive Regimes	Workers' Rights	Code of Conduct	Irresponsible Marketing	Armaments	Genetic Engineering	Boycott Call	Political Donations	
ACER	●	●	●	●	●	●	●	○	●	●	●	●	●		●	Pan Acer Group
AMD	○	●	●	○	●	●	●	○	●	●	●	●	●		●	AMD Inc
APPLE	○	●	●	●	●	●	●	●	○	●	●	●	●		●	Apple Computers Inc
COMPAQ	○	●	●	○	●	●	●	●	●	●	●	●	○		●	Hewlett Packard Co
CYRIX / C3	●	●	●	●	●	●	●	●	●	●	●	●	●		●	Via Technologies Inc
DELL	○	●	●	●	●	●	●	○	●	●	●	●	●		●	Dell Technology Holdings
EVESHAM	●	●	●	●	●	●	●	●	●	●	●	●	●		●	Evesham Technologies Ltd
FUJITSU	●	●	●	●	●	●	●	○	○	●	●	●	●		●	Dai Ichi Kangyo/Siemens AG
HEWLETT-PACKARD	○	●	●	○	●	●	●	●	●	●	●	●	○		●	Hewlett Packard Co
IBM	●	●	●	●	●	●	●	●	●	●	●	●	●		●	IBM Corp
INTEL	●	●	●	●	●	●	●	●	○	●	●	●	●	●USA		Intel Corp
NEC	●	●	●	●	●	●	●	●	○	●	●	●	●		●	Sumitomo Group
PACKARD BELL	●	●	●	●	●	●	●	●	○	●	●	●	●		●	Sumitomo Group
SIEMENS	●	●	●	●	●	●	●	●	○	●	●	●	●		●	Siemens AG/Dai Ichi Kangyo
SONY	●	●	●	●	●	●	●	●	●	●	●	●	●		●	Sony Corp
SUN	○	●	●	●	●	●	●	○	○	●	●	○	●		●	Sun Microsystems
TIME	●	●	●	●	●	●	●	●	●	●	●	●	●		●	Time Group Ltd
TINY	●	●	●	●	●	●	●	●	●	●	●	●	●		●	Time Group Ltd
TOSHIBA	●	●	●	○	●	●	●	●	○	●	●	●	○		●	Mitsui Group
VIGLEN	●	●	●	●	●	●	●	●	●	●	●	●	●		●	Learning Technology Plc

Key

● Top rating (no criticisms found)

○ Middle rating

● Bottom rating

● A related company has a bottom rating and the company itself has a middle rating

○ A related company has a middle rating

● A related company has a bottom rating

Source: ECRA-See page 14 for full key to symbols.

Fax machines

The fax machine has been one of the few survivors from the early communications revolution of the 1980s. Even the ever-growing use of email has not taken away the usefulness of the fax as a quick way to transfer pictures, sketches, maps etc – the sorts of things that can take time to download on the internet. At the same time, plain paper fax machines which can also scan, print and copy are increasingly popular with small businesses and home offices. When considering such a machine, we need to give a thought to conservation and the other things the manufacturers get up to.

TYPES OF PAPER

Plain paper machines use ordinary sheets of A4 paper while thermal fax machines use rolls of thermal paper. On the face of it, plain paper machines seem the better option, but two factors are worth thinking about: (i) a plain paper machine also requires a replaceable ink or toner cartridge or drum; (ii) a thermal fax machine cuts messages to length and thus saves on paper and energy.

Plain paper made from 100 per cent post-consumer waste is widely available. Look for the Nordic Swan symbol, a Scandinavian labelling scheme which requires the production process to have the minimum possible environmental impact. Thermal paper, contrary to popular opinion, is recyclable, although it is considered 'low-grade' waste and there are no known sources of recycled thermal paper.

The computer solution is to send and receive faxes without the use of paper, but you can only fax material which is stored in the computer and so a scanner is likely to be necessary. The drawback is that computers cannot receive faxes when they are switched off or when we are working offline.

COMPANIES' OTHER POLICIES

At the time of this report, four companies – BT, Samsung, Canon and Panasonic – were selling the most fax machines in the UK. BT's machines were mainly made by the French company Sagem. The main manufacturers were international electronics and office equipment companies, half of them from Japan, with two of them – Canon and NEC – belonging to the prevailing coalitions of Japanese multinationals. It can be seen from the long table on page 61 Several of the companies were involved in armaments or nuclear power.

Two environmental reports received top rating on the EC table. The BT report was accepted as a model of environmental reporting, showing progress against previous environmental targets, and reporting a 'green procurement' programme, taking into account its own suppliers' environmental objectives in its purchasing decisions. NEC similarly reported on performance against targets and operated a green procurement programme, although environmental audits were undertaken internally.

GOOD SHOPPING GUIDE 2003 ETHICAL
- Brother
- Olivetti
- Ricoh

- Sagem
- Samsung

- BT
- Canon
- NEC
- Panasonic

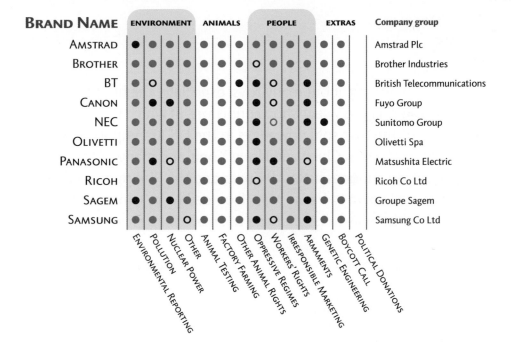

BRAND NAME	ENVIRONMENT	ANIMALS	PEOPLE	EXTRAS	Company group
AMSTRAD					Amstrad Plc
BROTHER					Brother Industries
BT					British Telecommunications
CANON					Fuyo Group
NEC					Sunitomo Group
OLIVETTI					Olivetti Spa
PANASONIC					Matsushita Electric
RICOH					Ricoh Co Ltd
SAGEM					Groupe Sagem
SAMSUNG					Samsung Co Ltd

Column headings (left to right): ENVIRONMENTAL REPORTING, POLLUTION, NUCLEAR POWER, OTHER, ANIMAL TESTING, FACTORY FARMING, OTHER ANIMAL RIGHTS, OPPRESSIVE REGIMES, WORKERS' RIGHTS, IRRESPONSIBLE MARKETING, ARMAMENTS, GENETIC ENGINEERING, BOYCOTT CALL, POLITICAL DONATIONS

Key

- ● Top rating (no criticisms found)
- ○ Middle rating
- ● Bottom rating
- ◉ A related company has a bottom rating and the company itself has a middle rating
- ○ A related company has a middle rating
- ● A related company has a bottom rating

Source: ECRA-See page 14 for full key to symbols.

Toys

What's most worrying about many toys, especially the brightest and noisiest of them, is the sweat-shop conditions in which they may be made. Most of the toys sold nowadays in the UK are imported – more than half of them from China and Hong Kong, and many of the rest from Taiwan, Thailand, Indonesia, South Korea and the Philippines, where regulations are known to be lax. We also need to be concerned about the use of PVC, which may cause damage to small children when it is chewed.

WORKING CONDITIONS

Examples of the poor working conditions within toy factories are unfortunately numerous, from 17-year-olds in China working 11-hour days for just a few pounds a week, to children under the age of 15 making toys until 11 o'clock at night. There was one terrible incident in 1993 when a fire broke out at the Kader toy factory in Thailand. It quickly consumed the building leaving 188 dead and 500 injured. A government study later confirmed that poor safety measures, such as a lack of fire exits and locked doors and windows, had played a major part in the disaster.

A World Development Movement (WDM) campaign has tried to persuade manufacturers to adopt codes of conduct about working conditions in the factories they source from, but with limited success. Some companies do have codes of their own. Mattel's code promises not to employ forced or child labour, but the most comprehensive code is Lego's which complies with most of WDM's demands.

THE PVC PROBLEM

Greenpeace has long campaigned for a ban on the use of PVC plastics in toys, citing evidence that phthalates (hazardous chemicals added to PVC to make it soft and flexible) may leach out when toys are chewed. PVC also generates hazardous chlorinated emissions and wastes.

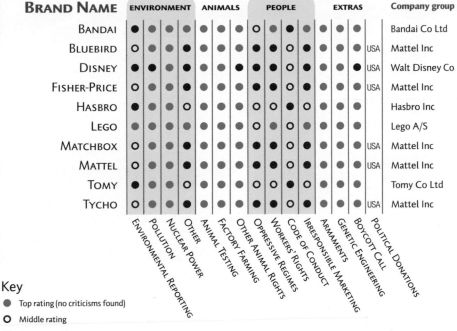

BRAND NAME	ENVIRONMENT				ANIMALS			PEOPLE				EXTRAS				Company group
BANDAI																Bandai Co Ltd
BLUEBIRD															USA	Mattel Inc
DISNEY															USA	Walt Disney Co
FISHER-PRICE															USA	Mattel Inc
HASBRO																Hasbro Inc
LEGO																Lego A/S
MATCHBOX															USA	Mattel Inc
MATTEL															USA	Mattel Inc
TOMY																Tomy Co Ltd
TYCHO															USA	Mattel Inc

Column headers (diagonal):
ENVIRONMENTAL REPORTING, POLLUTION, NUCLEAR POWER, OTHER, ANIMAL TESTING, FACTORY FARMING, OTHER ANIMAL RIGHTS, OPPRESSIVE REGIMES, WORKERS' RIGHTS, CODE OF CONDUCT, IRRESPONSIBLE MARKETING, ARMAMENTS, GENETIC ENGINEERING, BOYCOTT CALL, POLITICAL DONATIONS

Key

- Top rating (no criticisms found)
- ○ Middle rating
- Bottom rating
- A related company has a bottom rating and the company itself has a middle rating
- ○ A related company has a middle rating
- A related company has a bottom rating

Source: ECRA-See page 14 for full key to symbols.

GOOD SHOPPING GUIDE 2003 ETHICAL
- Bandai
- Lego

?
- Hasbro
- Tomy

✕
- Bluebird
- Disney
- Fisher-Price
- Matchbox
- Mattel
- Tycho

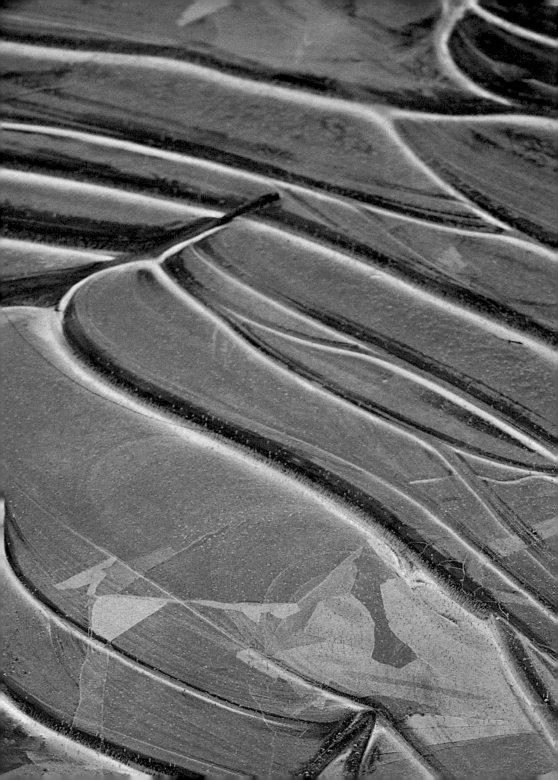

Washing-up liquid

When we clean our dishes effortlessly how can we be sure we're not making the planet that much dirtier? We would be well advised to look for liquids derived from vegetable sources rather than from highly-polluting petrochemical plants.

INGREDIENTS

The active ingredient in washing-up liquid is its surfactant, which allows grease to be removed more quickly by emulsifying oils and keeping them dispersed and suspended so they don't settle back onto the surface. The most commonly found surfactants in hand dishwashing detergents are 'anionic' which usually means they create a lot of suds. Some products also list ionic or non-ionic surfactants.

All the surfactants may also be produced from vegetable oils (such as coconut) as well as from petrochemical sources, but only the eco-friendly products use the vegetable-based or 'oleo' surfactants. Faith Products, Bio-D, Little Green Shop, Down to Earth, Caurnie and Ecover are among these. In a life cycle inventory study by a German research body, the oleo surfactants were shown to be better than petrochemical surfactants in 9 of the 13 categories studied. The petrochemical surfactants were found to be slower to biodegrade and they were significantly more damaging in terms of aquatic and air eco-toxicity, global warming, depletion of water, acidification, petrochemical oxidant formation and consumption of renewable energy sources.

Synthetic perfume and colourings, also based on petrochemicals, can be slow to degrade and may cause problems for those with sensitive skin. The 'green' brands tend to be colourless and use natural fragrances such as volatile plant oils.

ANTIBACTERIAL ADDITIVES

Procter & Gamble launched Fairy Antibacterial in 1997, which it claims helps kill E-coli, salmonella and campylobacter. Others, including supermarket own brands, have followed with their own disinfectant formulas. Proper cooking and basic kitchen hygiene offer complete protection for everyone.

PACKAGING

Most washing-up liquid bottles are made of high-density polyethylene (labelled PE or HDPE). This is one of the few plastics that is beginning to be recycled in the UK, although provision of local collection schemes is patchy. Bio-D's bottles contain 55 per cent recycled material, which according to a company spokesperson is the maximum possible without the plastic becoming too brittle. Ecover and Bio-D are the only companies providing natural products suppliers with large drums that allow customers to refill their bottles regularly.

ALTERNATIVES

In a hard water area it is a good idea to use a water softener so that we can reduce the amount of suds we generate. Some people even recycle good old-fashioned soap to make a perfectly good washing-up liquid, by saving old soap scraps in a jar and mixing them up in boiling water. Try and buy *Good Shopping Guide* ethical brands when you can – it's a key area.

- Bio-D
- Caurnie
- Clear Spring
- Ecover
- Little Green Shop

- Morning Fresh
- Surcare

- Ajax
- Fairy
- Palmolive
- Persil

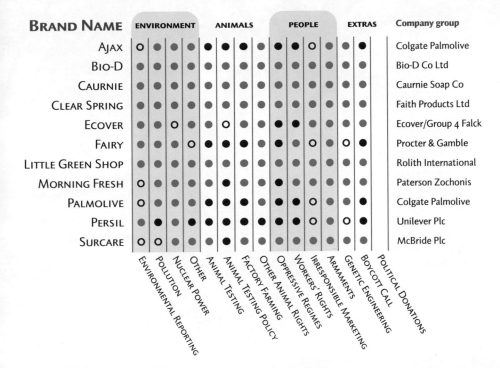

BRAND NAME	Company group
AJAX	Colgate Palmolive
BIO-D	Bio-D Co Ltd
CAURNIE	Caurnie Soap Co
CLEAR SPRING	Faith Products Ltd
ECOVER	Ecover/Group 4 Falck
FAIRY	Procter & Gamble
LITTLE GREEN SHOP	Rolith International
MORNING FRESH	Paterson Zochonis
PALMOLIVE	Colgate Palmolive
PERSIL	Unilever Plc
SURCARE	McBride Plc

Column categories — ENVIRONMENT, ANIMALS, PEOPLE, EXTRAS:

Environmental Reporting, Pollution, Nuclear Power, Other, Animal Testing, Animal Testing Policy, Factory Farming, Other Animal Rights, Oppressive Regimes, Workers' Rights, Irresponsible Marketing, Armaments, Genetic Engineering, Boycott Call, Political Donations

Key

- Top rating (no criticisms found)
- Middle rating
- Bottom rating
- A related company has a bottom rating and the company itself has a middle rating
- A related company has a middle rating
- A related company has a bottom rating

Source: ECRA-See page 14 for full key to symbols.

Laundry detergents

Whiter, brighter and smarter! But are we making our environment any cleaner as we endlessly chuck our scarcely-worn shirts, socks and underwear into the washing machine, throw in some liquid or powder, click the switch and forget about it? Unlikely! The very fact that every day is washing day for most families means that, collectively, we are using far more energy, water and detergents than ever before in history.

To be sure of not damaging the environment excessively, we should be thinking about the more eco-friendly products. Have a good look at the tables overleaf.

OVER-PERFORMANCE

The research and development divisions of the mega-wash companies – Procter & Gamble and Lever Brothers churn over 84 per cent of British clothes in the wash every day – have come up with ever-more impressive-sounding formulations, leaving most of us poor consumers simply spinning with confusion. Understandably, most of us are indeed interested in performance and value for money, but we should think about whether we really need to have the highest level of performance for the simple things we put in the wash – which really only need freshening rather than a full wash that goes the whole hog with biological ingredients and all.

INGREDIENTS TO WATCH

We should definitely watch out for the quantity of surfactants that we get through – and these are still in all the products from the mega-wash companies, together with

60-SECOND GREEN GUIDE

- For mainstream brands, a washing powder is better than a liquid, and a concentrated powder better than a standard powder
- Use soap-based detergents, or ones with a high soap content
- Vegetable-based surfactants are better than petrochemical based ones
- Use a product without phosphates, phosphonates or carboxylates
- You can make eco-products work better in hard water areas by using a water softener
- Choose a low wash temperature, or select the 'economy' cycle if your machine has one

ingredients like phosphates, phosphonates and carboxylates. For those concerned about enzymes, these are not bad for the environment, but there have been problems for workers in the factories making them – which seem largely to have been sorted out by now.

Anyone who has tried the ecological brands like Ecover and Bio-D will have noticed that they can be less efficient at removing the most stubborn stains, although they do dispense with the most environmentally damaging ingredients of the mega-wash products, especially their petrochemical-based surfactants.

AN EFFICIENT BALANCE

Having carefully considered the best trade-offs between efficiency and environmental impacts, ECRA recommends the following combination for handling the majority of our clothes:

- Ecover or Bio-D (or equivalent) for a regular detergent wash
- Biological powder for a quarterly zapping of the dirtiest items

- ACDO
- Advance (Tesco)
- Bio-D
- Clear Spring
- Co-op
- Cyclon (Safeway)
- Ecover
- Logic (ASDA)
- Novon (Sainsbury)
- Surcare

- Ariel
- Bold
- Daz
- Dreft
- Fairy

- Persil
- Surf

BRAND NAME	ENVIRONMENT	ANIMALS	PEOPLE	EXTRAS	Company group
ACDO					ACDOCO Ltd
ADVANCE (TESCO)					McBride Plc
ARIEL					Procter & Gamble
BIO-D					Bio-D Co. Ltd
BOLD					Procter & Gamble
CLEAR SPRING					Faith Products Ltd
CO-OP					McBride Plc
CYCLON (SAFEWAY)					McBride Plc
DAZ					Procter & Gamble
DREFT					Procter & Gamble
ECOVER					Ecover/Group 4 Falck
FAIRY					Procter & Gamble
LOGIC (ASDA)					McBride Plc
NOVON (SAINSBURY)					McBride Plc
PERSIL					Unilever Plc
SURCARE					McBride Plc
SURF					Unilever Plc

Rating categories (columns, left to right):

ENVIRONMENTAL REPORTING · POLLUTION · NUCLEAR POWER · OTHER · ANIMAL TESTING · ANIMAL TESTING POLICY · FACTORY FARMING · OTHER ANIMAL RIGHTS · OPPRESSIVE REGIMES · WORKERS RIGHTS · IRRESPONSIBLE MARKETING · ARMAMENTS · GENETIC ENGINEERING · BOYCOTT CALL · POLITICAL DONATIONS

Key

- ● Top rating (no criticisms found)
- ○ Middle rating
- ● Bottom rating
- ◖ A related company has a bottom rating and the company itself has a middle rating
- ○ A related company has a middle rating
- ● A related company has a bottom rating

Source: ECRA-See page 14 for full key to symbols.

Household cleaning products

In every supermarket there is a bewildering display of creams, scourers, liquids, sprays and mousses, all promising to keep our bathrooms, kitchens and houses sparkling clean and free from all possible bacteria. How much of the hype should we believe? And how much of this stuff do we really need?

CHEMICALS AND POLLUTION

Fifty years ago, common cleaning substances were close to those recommended in the Alternatives section listed here – i.e. simple scouring powders, soap-based detergents etc. Products have become increasingly complex (multi-surface cleaners, toilet fresheners) and petrochemical-based ingredients have taken over. Brand names have proliferated – and while there are now legal and voluntary controls on the most harmful chemicals, any improvements are still being offset by increases in the sheer quantities of these products that people use. Many of today's cleaning products contain chemicals that contribute to aquatic pollution when they drain into rivers. Greater quantities of bleach and detergent are discharged directly into sewers from homes than from the factories making them.

Certain manufacturers attempt to use safer ingredients to avoid the risk of their accumulation in the environment. Such consciously green brands as Ecover and Bio-D, confident of having nothing to hide, tend to list all of their ingredients.

CLEANERS AND DETERGENTS

Several types of bleach exist, all of which act by oxidising, and thus sterilising, organic matter. Its powerful antibacterial action has been seen to persist beyond the U-bend, undermining the bacterial action that helps break down sewage. For this reason it should be used in dilute form, if at all, and never be poured neat down drains. Neither Ecover nor Bio-D produce household bleach, because they believe the action is unnecessarily powerful. Their toilet cleaners rely on acids.

Most detergents are based on 'surfactants', chemicals which cut through grease and dirt, allowing them to disperse in water. They can also increase the penetration of other harmful chemicals into living things by damaging their protective layers, even, it is thought, at low concentrations. Research has shown that a concentration of one part per million of some surfactants can have a lethal effect on frogspawn. It is essential that detergents are biodegradable. The vegetable oil-based surfactants used by green detergent-makers will be quicker to biodegrade than the non-organic kind, although companies would

World Development Movement

Dedicated to tackling the root causes of world poverty

Making world trade work for the world's poor

Campaigning to end the injustice of third world debt

We are winning changes for a better world

Join us!

www.wdm.org.uk
0800 328 2153

WORLD
DEVELOPMENT
MOVEMENT

Because a better world is possible

Batteries

Much of our day-to-day equipment is battery-driven – especially those things we carry around daily like watches, mobiles and cameras – and the batteries are so small they might seem harmless. So can anyone blame us when we throw our batteries into the bin? But before we do, we need to check on the potential damage to the environment.

TOXIC INGREDIENTS

Batteries inevitably contain some degree of either toxic or corrosive chemicals but the manufacturers and environmental groups have so far failed to find much common ground in their debates about production and disposal. Until these issues are fully cleared up, we should at least look for the products with the lowest impact on the environment.

Nickel Cadmium batteries, or NiCads, are the ones most often sold as 'rechargeable', a fact that rightly attracts environmentally-concerned consumers, but NiCads do contain cadmium, which is a highly toxic heavy metal. To get over this problem, the five main manufacturers – Eveready, Panasonic, Rayovac, Uniross and Varta – do have facilities to collect their own brand NiCads and to send them for recycling, if we make the effort to send them in when completely used up.

Nickel metal hydride (NiMH) batteries avoid the cadmium problem but, at the time of the EC survey, they were available only as battery packs for camcorders, computers and mobile phones. As these become more widespread, it can only be

hoped that the manufacturers will put in place proper recycling arrangements that their customers will understand and want to adhere to.

Zinc and alkaline batteries are rechargeable, but far less effectively than NiCads, and the real problem is that there are virtually no facilities to recycle them, at least in the UK. Although the industry maintains that the impact on landfills is negligible, environmentalists are convinced that they will leave problem chemicals in the ground for future generations to deal with.

OTHER TYPES

Button cells are the small flat batteries used in watches, hearing aids and some cameras. The formulations include lithium, zinc air, silver oxide and alkaline. Previously they used mercuric oxide cells, but these have at last been phased out. If at all possible, lithium batteries should be avoided. If appropriate, silver oxide is the best option.

On the positive side, there have been considerable improvements in recent years, including the elimination of mercury and manufacturers' involvement in collecting NiCads from larger commercial users of power tools, mobile phones and emergency lighting.

WHAT NEXT?

The ideal situation would be the collection and recycling of all battery waste. For the industry this would mean proper labelling and establishment of recycling schemes for all batteries. For consumers, the message should be to buy rechargeable batteries from retailers that promise to accept back and recycle them, whether as single batteries or packs.

- Energizer
- Ever Ready
- Rayovac
- Uniross

- Duracell
- Kodak
- Philips
- Varta

- Boots
- Panasonic
- Sony

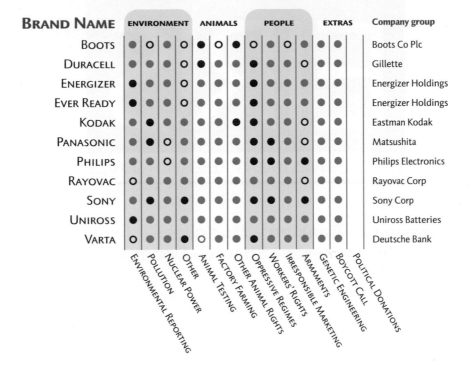

BRAND NAME	ENVIRONMENT	ANIMALS	PEOPLE	EXTRAS	Company group
Boots					Boots Co Plc
Duracell					Gillette
Energizer					Energizer Holdings
Ever Ready					Energizer Holdings
Kodak					Eastman Kodak
Panasonic					Matsushita
Philips					Philips Electronics
Rayovac					Rayovac Corp
Sony					Sony Corp
Uniross					Uniross Batteries
Varta					Deutsche Bank

Column headings (left to right): ENVIRONMENTAL REPORTING, POLLUTION, NUCLEAR POWER, OTHER, ANIMAL TESTING, FACTORY FARMING, OTHER ANIMAL RIGHTS, OPPRESSIVE REGIMES, WORKERS' RIGHTS, IRRESPONSIBLE MARKETING, ARMAMENTS, GENETIC ENGINEERING, BOYCOTT CALL, POLITICAL DONATIONS

Key

- Top rating (no criticisms found)
- Middle rating
- Bottom rating
- A related company has a bottom rating and the company itself has a middle rating
- A related company has a middle rating
- A related company has a bottom rating

Source: ECRA–See page 14 for full key to symbols.

ETHICAL INVESTMENT RESEARCH SERVICE

**Pensions – Banking – Mortgages – Insurance
Investments - Shares - Donations**

Do you know where your money is going?

Do you know who you are funding?

**EIRIS is a leading independent research provider
for socially responsible investors. Established in
1983 we are dedicated to helping people invest
according to their principles.**

For further information contact EIRIS at:

**80-84 Bondway, London SW8 1SF
Tel 020 7840 5700
Fax 020 7735 5323
Email ethics@eiris.org
Visit www.eiris.org**

EIRIS does not give financial or investment advice, but can indicate financial advisers and
fund managers who specialise in ethical or socially responsible investment.

Good Money

Charity credit cards

Charity affinity credit cards are excellent, because they continually raise money for good causes without serious cost to the customer. Nowadays, there are plenty on offer, most of which let us choose which charities we wish to support. Single charities issue the cards both for raising money and winning publicity. Several banks co-operate closely with them, but not all. Read here for details.

BENEFITS

A charity credit card raises money for a charity (or several) when the card is first taken out or first used, and from then on a small percentage, like 25p for every £100 used, goes straight to the charity. The charities benefit from the extra revenue and also because the cards and associated marketing can raise their profile and thus recruit new members.

Few affinity cards charge an annual fee, but it is worth checking on this before taking one. Some have low introductory rates of interest in the first few months, but in general the rates are close to the average available at any one time. This is irrelevant if we pay off our bill in full, as most affinity cardholders apparently do. As the donations depend on the money spent, not on the size of the outstanding balance, there is no loss to the charity if we do clear it every month.

Many banks have been happy to co-operate not only with conventional charities but also with sports clubs, hobby groups and professional organisations,

seeing it as a way to gain market share. In terms of ethics, it makes little difference whether our card is Visa or Mastercard. It is more appropriate to ask which bank the charity has teamed up with to issue its credit card. Some of the banks have resisted getting involved, considering cards too costly to administer or being reluctant to pay VAT on donations.

BANKS

Of the UK high street banks, Bank of Scotland, Royal Bank of Scotland, Halifax, Co-operative and HSBC all offer charity-linked cards. Three US banks, MBNA, Beneficial and People's Bank of Connecticut, jointly issue affinity cards with charities.

Co-op Bank cards support among others Amnesty International, Greenpeace, Help the Aged, Save the Children, Oxfam and the RSPB. Beneficial Bank has several cards which benefit animal welfare charities as well as the Wildlife and

Wetlands Trust, English Heritage and Unicef. Frizzell supports the Cancer Research Campaign, while People's Bank has cards for Comic Relief and the Vegetarian Society. The Bank of Scotland also has several to choose from.

THE PVC ISSUE

Co-operative Bank has been researching alternatives to PVC for its credit and debit cards and hopes to make a biodegradable plastic known as polyethylene teraphthalate, completely free of hazardous chemicals. No other UK card issuers seem to have followed their lead.

GOOD SHOPPING GUIDE 2003 ETHICAL

- Beneficial Bank
- Co-operative Bank
- Frizzell Bank
- People's Bank

- Bank of Scotland
- Halifax
- MBNA

- HSBC
- Royal Bank of Scotland

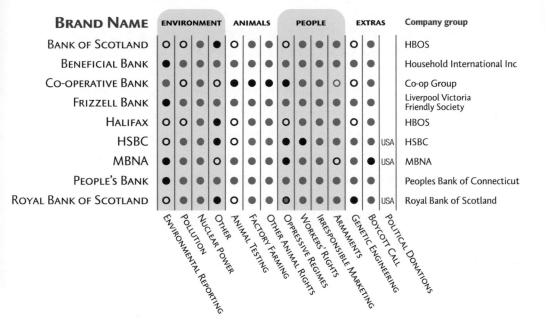

BRAND NAME	ENVIRONMENT				ANIMALS			PEOPLE				EXTRAS			Company group
	Environmental Reporting	Pollution	Nuclear Power	Other	Animal Testing	Factory Farming	Other Animal Rights	Oppressive Regimes	Workers' Rights	Irresponsible Marketing	Armaments	Genetic Engineering	Boycott Call	Political Donations	
BANK OF SCOTLAND	○	○	●	●	○	●	●	○	●	●	●	○	●		HBOS
BENEFICIAL BANK	●	●	●	●	●	●	●	●	●	●	●	●	●		Household International Inc
CO-OPERATIVE BANK	●	○	●	○	●	●	●	●	●	●	○	○	●		Co-op Group
FRIZZELL BANK	●	●	●	●	●	●	●	●	●	●	●	●	●		Liverpool Victoria Friendly Society
HALIFAX	○	○	●	●	○	●	●	○	●	●	●	○	●		HBOS
HSBC	○	●	●	●	○	●	●	●	●	●	●	●	●	USA	HSBC
MBNA	●	●	●	○	●	●	●	●	●	●	○	●	●	USA	MBNA
PEOPLE'S BANK	●	●	●	●	●	●	●	●	●	●	●	●	●		Peoples Bank of Connecticut
ROYAL BANK OF SCOTLAND	○	●	●	●	○	●	●	●	●	●	●	●	●	USA	Royal Bank of Scotland

Key

● Top rating (no criticisms found)

○ Middle rating

● Bottom rating

● A related company has a bottom rating and the company itself has a middle rating

○ A related company has a middle rating

● A related company has a bottom rating

Source: ECRA-See page 14 for full key to symbols.

Banks & Building Societies

Banks and building societies claim to have their customers' interests at heart, but are they really listening? Most of us choose our banks or building societies for reasons of convenience – simply because there's a branch around the corner or maybe because we had an account with a predecessor of one of today's conglomerates. But, as customers, we have the right to make judgements about the ways our banks behave, not least in the realm of their relationships with the developing world.

THE MUTUAL ISSUE

Support mutual building societies like Britannia. This specifically excludes de-mutualised building societies – those that have become banks – such as the Alliance & Leicester, Halifax, Northern Rock and Bradford & Bingley. The debate over the future of mutual building societies has largely focused on their potential benefits to customers; mutual status means that there are no shareholders to pay dividends to, so profits can be ploughed back into lower loans charges and higher interest rates for savers. These claims appear to be borne out by *Which?* magazine's July 2001 study, which reported that in general, mutuals still give better deals on mortgages and savings than their de-mutualised cousins.

Some mutual building societies can also offer a better option than most banks as they don't take business customers, so they could never fund dubious business practices, like logging or oil exploration. Of those on the table, the Coventry, Yorkshire, Leeds & Holbeck and Portman do not lend commercially. Information on the benefits of mutuals, and a list of the remaining mutual building societies, can be obtained from the Building Societies Association on 020 7437 0655 or *www.bsa.org.uk*

THIRD WORLD CONCERNS

Several British banks – most notably Lloyds (now Lloyds TSB) and Midland (now HSBC) – were the focus of campaigns in the 1980s and 90s over their holdings of Third World debt. Much of this has now been written off as banks realised that they were unlikely to recoup the loans, and that they were acquiring significant bad publicity. Some, such as the Bank of Scotland, 'swapped' their poorest-country debts for commitments by national governments that they would use the money for domestic development programmes. However, EIRIS has listed some high street banks as still holding some Third World debt. See *eiris.org*.

British banks have been the targets of

other important campaigns about their holding of World Bank bonds, their involvement in the kind of currency speculation that has ruined many developing countries, and their support for the World Trade Organisation's controversial agreement on trade and services. Some of these issues are indicated in the table.

ETHICAL HEALTH CHECK

Information on the environmental and social policies and reporting standards of a range of banks can be found in an EIRIS factsheet, available from 0845 606 0324 or *www.eiris.org*

- Abbey National
- Alliance & Leicester
- Bradford & Bingley
- Britannia BS
- Chelsea BS
- Chesire BS
- Co-op Bank
- Coventry BS
- Derbyshire BS
- Girobank
- Leeds & Holbeck
- Nationwide BS
- Northern Rock
- Norwich & Peterborough
- Portman BS
- Skipton BS
- Yorkshire BS
- Other Mutuals

- Bank of Scotland
- Barclays Bank
- Clydesdale Bank
- Egg
- Halifax
- Lloyds TSB
- National Australia Bank
- Safeway
- Woolwich
- Yorkshire Bank

- ASDA
- Bank of Ireland
- HSBC
- Morrisons
- National Westminster
- Royal Bank of Scotland
- Sainsbury's
- Tesco Plc
- Virgin Direct

Brand Name	ENVIRONMENT				ANIMALS			PEOPLE				EXTRAS				Company group
	Environmental Reporting	Pollution	Nuclear Power	Other	Animal Testing	Factory Farming	Other Animal Rights	Oppressive Regimes	Workers' Rights	Irresponsible Marketing	Armaments	Genetic Engineering	Boycott Call	Political Donations		
ABBEY NATIONAL	○	●	●	○	●	●	●	●	●	●	●	●	●			Abbey National Plc
ALLIANCE AND LEICESTER	○	●	●	○	●	●	●	●	●	●	●	●	●			Alliance & Leicester
ASDA	●	◐	○	●	●	●	●	◐	●	◐	○	○	●	USA		Wal-Mart/Lloyds TSB
BANK OF IRELAND	○	●	●	○	●	●	●	●	●	●	●	●	○	USA		Bank of Ireland
BANK OF SCOTLAND	○	○	●	●	○	●	●	○	●	●	●	○	●			HBOS
BARCLAYS	●	●	●	●	○	●	●	●	●	●	●	○	●	CON		Barclays Plc
BRADFORD & BINGLEY	●	●	●	●	●	●	●	●	●	●	●	●	●			Bradford & Bingley
BRITANNIA BS	●	●	●	●	●	●	●	●	●	●	●	●	●			Britannia BS
CHELSEA BS	●	●	●	●	●	●	●	●	●	●	●	●	●			Chelsea BS
CHESHIRE BS	●	●	●	●	●	●	●	●	●	●	●	●	●			Cheshire BS
CITIBANK	○	●	●	●	○	●	●	●	●	●	●	○	●	USA		Citigroup
CLYDESDALE	●	●	●	●	●	●	○	◐	●	●	○	●	○	LAB		National Australia Bank
CO-OP BANK	●	○	●	○	●	●	●	●	●	●	○	○	●			Co-operative Group
COVENTRY BS	●	●	●	●	●	●	●	●	●	●	●	●	●			Coventry BS
DERBYSHIRE BS	○	●	●	●	●	●	●	●	●	●	●	●	●			Derbyshire BS
EGG	○	●	●	●	●	●	●	○	●	●	●	●	●			Prudential
GIROBANK	○	●	●	○	●	●	●	●	●	●	●	●	●			Alliance & Leicester
HALIFAX	○	○	●	●	○	●	●	○	●	●	●	○	●			HBOS

Key

- ● Top rating (no criticisms found)
- ○ Middle rating
- ● Bottom rating
- ◐ A related company has a bottom rating and the company itself has a middle rating
- ○ A related company has a middle rating
- ● A related company has a bottom rating

Source: ECRA-See page 14 for full key to symbols.

NB The amber, related company marks, relate to companies which are customers of the banks in question. So if a particular company has been found guilty of pollution, its bank will receive an amber mark.

Brand Name	ENVIRONMENT				ANIMALS			PEOPLE				EXTRAS				Company group
	Environmental Reporting	Pollution	Nuclear Power	Other	Animal Testing	Factory Farming	Other Animal Rights	Oppressive Regimes	Workers' Rights	Irresponsible Marketing	Armaments	Genetic Engineering	Boycott Call	Political Donations		
HSBC	O	●	●	●	O	●	●	●	●	●	●	●		●	USA	HSBC Plc
Leeds & Holbeck	●	●	●	●	●	●	●	●	●	●	●	●		●		Leeds & Holbeck BS
Lloyds TSB	O	●	O	O	O	●	●	●	◐	●	●	O		●	USA	Lloyds TSB
Morrisons	●	●	●	●	●	●	●	●	●	●	●	◐		●	USA	WMorrison/HSBC
Nationwide	●	●	●	●	●	●	●	●	●	●	●	●		●		Nationwide BS
NatWest	O	●	●	●	O	●	●	◐	●	●	●	●		●	USA	Royal Bank of Scotland
Northern Rock	O	●	●	●	●	●	●	●	●	●	●	●		●		Northern Rock Plc
Norwich & Peterboro'	O	●	●	●	●	●	●	●	●	●	●	●		●		Norwich & Peterborough BS
Portman BS	●	●	●	●	●	●	●	●	●	●	●	●		●		Portman BS
RBS	O	●	●	●	O	●	●	◐	●	●	●	●		●	USA	Royal Bank of Scotland
Safeway	O	●	●	●	●	●	●	O	●	O	●	O		●		Safeway Plc/Abbey National
Sainsbury's	O	●	●	●	●	●	●	O	O	O	O	O		●	LAB	J Sainsbury/HBOS
Skipton BS	●	●	●	●	●	●	●	●	●	●	●	●		●		Skipton BS
Tesco	●	●	●	●	●	●	●	◐	●	●	●	●		●	USA	Tesco/RBS
Virgin Direct	●	●	●	●	O	●	●	●	◐	●	●	●		●	USA	Virgin/RBS
Woolwich	●	●	●	●	O	●	●	●	●	●	●	O		●	CON	Barclays Plc
Yorkshire Bank	●	●	●	●	●	●	O	◐	●	●	O	●		O	LAB	National Australia Bank
Yorkshire BS	●	●	●	●	O	●	●	●	●	●	●	●		●		Yorkshire BS

NB The amber, related company marks, relate to companies which are customers of the banks in question. So if a particular company has been found guilty of pollution, its bank will recieve an amber mark.

89

Insurance

Choosing insurance companies is rather like a lottery. They may be offering the best deal today but who knows what will happen in the future? Companies keep merging and taking each other over and sometimes we can hardly tell their names apart. One way to keep ahead of the main companies at least is to look at their ethical policies and to ask questions about the kinds of companies that the insurance managers like to invest in.

POWER OF THE COMPANIES

Insurance companies are so rich that they are estimated to own around 16 per cent of the UK stock market. Their investments are often in companies that may be controversial, as Monsanto and Shell have been at different times. Campaigners have become increasingly impatient over unethical corporate activities and they are learning how to put pressure on insurance companies as shareholders. One way to make this pressure work is to keep consumers aware of what their insurers are investing in.

ENVIRONMENTAL PRESSURE

Campaigners do not always demand that problem company shares be sold but rather ask the insurance companies to use their power as shareholders to vote or create pressure for more ethical or environmentally sound behaviour by the target company. In 1999, Friends of the Earth (FoE) reported on the investment practices of Britain's top 14 life insurance firms, looking at the extent to which each had invested in companies criticised for causing environmental damage. The main argument was that the insurance industry would be a major casualty of the environmental practices of those they invest in, especially as the costs to insurers of compensation for losses caused by so-called 'natural' disasters is rising fast. FoE urged the insurance companies to push companies to improve their environmental record and pressed governments to introduce mandatory environmental reporting by companies.

A United Nations Environment Programme statement of commitment by the insurance industry was signed by around 30 companies in 1996 but this was not followed up by the major insurers. The signatories pledged to 'actively communicate environmental activities to the public' and to 'manage internal operations and physical assets under (their) control in a manner that reflects environmental considerations.'

ECRA DEMANDS

ECRA believes that the government should consider extending its ethical regulations for pension providers so that they apply to all large institutional investors, including the insurance industry. ECRA also believes that insurance companies should be obliged by law to disclose annually on their company website their 500 largest company shareholdings by value. This would permit an informed and accurate public debate about the ethical and environmental issues raised by specific holdings.

- AA
- Britannic
- Equitable Life
- Iron Trades
- Royal London

- Aegon
- Allied Dunbar
- Cornhill
- Eagle Star
- Prudential
- Scottish Amicable
- Scottish Equitable
- Standard Life
- Zurich

- AXA
- Clerical Medical
- Direct Line
- Legal & General
- Natwest
- Norwich Union
- Royal & Sun Alliance
- Scottish Widows

BRAND NAME	ENVIRONMENT				ANIMALS			PEOPLE				EXTRAS			Company group
	Environmental Reporting	Pollution	Nuclear Power	Other	Animal Testing	Factory Farming	Other Animal Rights	Oppressive Regimes	Workers' Rights	Irresponsible Marketing	Armaments	Genetic Engineering	Boycott Call	Political Donations	
AA	●	●	●	○	●	●	●	●	●	●	●	●	●		Automobile Association
AEGON	○	●	●	○	●	●	●	○	●	●	○	○	●		Aegon NV
ALLIED DUNBAR	○	●	○	●	○	●	●	●	●	●	●	○	●		Zurich Allied
AXA	●	●	●	○	●	●	●	●	○	●	●	●	●	CON	AXA-UAP
BRITANNIC	●	●	●	●	●	●	●	●	●	●	●	●	●		Britannic Insurance
CLERICAL MEDICAL	○	○	●	●	○	●	●	○	●	●	●	○	●		HBOS
CORNHILL	●	●	●	●	●	●	●	●	●	●	○	●	●		Allianz AC
DIRECT LINE	○	●	●	●	○	●	●	●	●	●	●	●	●	USA	Royal Bank of Scotland
EAGLE STAR	○	●	○	●	○	●	●	●	●	●	●	○	●		Zurich Allied
EQUITABLE LIFE	●	●	●	●	●	●	●	●	●	●	●	○	●		Equitable Life Assurance Society
IRON TRADES	○	●	●	●	●	●	●	○	●	●	●	●	●		QBE Insurance
LEGAL & GENERAL	○	●	●	●	●	●	●	○	●	●	●	○	●		Legal & General Group
NATWEST	○	●	●	●	○	●	●	●	●	●	●	●	●	USA	Royal Bank of Scotland
NORWICH UNION	○	●	●	●	●	●	●	●	●	●	●	●	●		CGNU
PRUDENTIAL	○	●	●	●	●	●	●	○	●	●	●	●	●		Prudential Corp Plc
ROYAL LONDON	●	●	●	●	●	●	●	●	●	●	●	●	●		Royal London Mutual
ROYAL & SUN ALLIANCE	○	●	●	●	●	●	●	●	●	●	●	○	●	CON	Royal & Sun Alliance
SCOTTISH AMICABLE	○	●	●	●	●	●	●	○	●	●	●	●	●		Prudential Corp
SCOTTISH EQUITABLE	○	●	●	○	●	●	●	○	●	●	○	○	●		Aegon NV
SCOTTISH WIDOWS	○	●	○	○	○	●	●	●	●	●	●	○	●	USA	Lloyds TSB
STANDARD LIFE	●	●	●	●	●	●	●	●	●	●	●	●	●		Standard Life Assurance Co
ZURICH	○	●	○	●	○	●	●	●	●	●	●	○	●		Zurich Allied

Key

● Top rating (no criticisms found)

○ Middle rating

● Bottom rating

◐ A related company has a bottom rating and the company itself has a middle rating

○ A related company has a middle rating

● A related company has a bottom rating

Source: ECRA-See page 14 for full key to symbols.

Mortgages

Ten years ago, most mortgages were taken out with building societies, but since de-mutualisation about four out of five mortgages are now provided by either a bank, a life insurer or a specialist mortgage lender. This section covers a few of the remaining building societies, some of the major bank lenders and some of the ethical mortgage lenders. All of the companies in the report offer standard 'repayment' mortgages.

WHY ETHICAL?

Mortgages are likely to be one of the single biggest outlays for many people. However, monthly repayments could be contributing to loans for animal testing laboratories or investment in companies involved in other unethical activities. Consequently, the mortgage company's lending policies are as important as the kind of mortgage on offer.

Although all the banks/building societies covered in this report were asked about their approach to lending, the only ones to offer comprehensive ethical lending policies were the Ecology Building Society and the Co-operative Bank. The Ecology lends primarily to 'green' housing and the Co-op excludes companies involved in a range of activities like animal testing and arms exports to oppressive regimes.

For companies which have not offered specific information, it is probably correct to assume that building societies are less likely than banks to be involved in what ECRA describes as 'questionable' corporate lending.

ENVIRONMENTAL ISSUES

Homes are one of the largest sources of carbon dioxide emissions in the UK. While most mortgage lenders offer valuation surveys as part of the mortgage deal, relatively few at this stage are offering specialised environmental surveys. These environmental surveys assess how energy efficient the house we want to buy is, and give advice on energy savings measures. Currently, the Co-op Bank offers this kind of survey free with its green mortgage, as do the Norwich & Peterborough and the Ethical Mortgage Service.

All the banks and building societies in this report were asked for their latest environmental reports. Although the situation has improved since EC last covered banks, few of the companies had any environmental report that would receive ECRA's clean rating. The Co-operative Bank continues to be a leader in this sector.

ETHICAL & GREEN MORTAGES

The Ecology Building Society currently lends only on properties that give 'ecological payback'. This translates as being houses which it considers energy-saving – such as back-to-backs, derelict houses which would otherwise have been abandoned, etc. This strict lending policy means that it won't be suitable to every person seeking a mortgage.

The Norwich & Peterborough offers a carbon-neutral mortgage. For the first five years of each of its Green Mortgages, it will plant eight trees a year. Its leaflet claims that the trees will absorb carbon dioxide to the equivalent of the estimated emissions of the property. It also offers a 'brown' mortgage scheme which aims to encourage the renovation and restoration of buildings for residential use.

The Co-operative Bank's green mortgage will 'pay Climate Care to offset around 20 per cent of an average home's carbon dioxide production for every mortgage we grant.' It claims over a 20-year mortgage, just under a fifth of an acre of forest would be planted.

The Ethical Mortgage Service is a collaboration between the Ethical Investment Co-operative (a group of Independent Financial Advisors) and consultants called Thirdwave. It offers advice on mortgages from a panel of lenders that it has ethically screened. This panel includes the Skipton, Scottish and Yorkshire Building Societies. For the purposes of this April/May 2001 report ECRA included the ratings for these building societies in the rating on the table for the Ethical Mortgage Service.

On the table, amber circles appear where the bank is an investor or service provider to companies criticised for particular activities.

- Abbey National
- Alliance & Leicester
- Co-op Bank
- Ecology BS
- Ethical Mortgage Service
- Nationwide
- Norwich & Peterborough

- Barclays
- Halifax plc
- Woolwich

- Cheltenham & Gloucester
- Lloyds TSB
- Natwest
- Royal Bank of Scotland

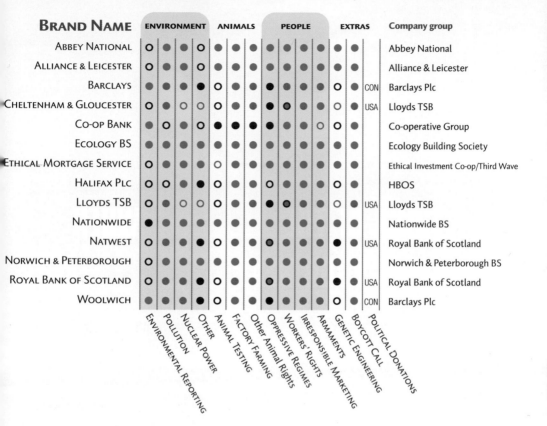

Brand Name	Environment				Animals			People				Extras			Company group
	Environmental Reporting	Pollution	Nuclear Power	Other	Animal Testing	Factory Farming	Other Animal Rights	Oppressive Regimes	Workers' Rights	Irresponsible Marketing	Armaments	Genetic Engineering	Boycott Call	Political Donations	
Abbey National	O	●	●	O	●	●	●	●	●	●	●	●	●		Abbey National
Alliance & Leicester	O	●	●	O	●	●	●	●	●	●	●	●	●		Alliance & Leicester
Barclays	●	●	●	●	O	●	●	●	●	●	●	O	●	CON	Barclays Plc
Cheltenham & Gloucester	O	●	O	O	O	●	●	●	●	●	●	O	●	USA	Lloyds TSB
Co-op Bank	●	O	●	O	●	●	●	●	●	●	O	O	●		Co-operative Group
Ecology BS	●	●	●	●	●	●	●	●	●	●	●	●	●		Ecology Building Society
Ethical Mortgage Service	O	●	●	●	O	●	●	●	●	●	●	●	●		Ethical Investment Co-op/Third Wave
Halifax Plc	O	O	●	●	O	●	●	O	●	●	●	O	●		HBOS
Lloyds TSB	O	●	O	O	O	●	●	●	●	●	●	O	●	USA	Lloyds TSB
Nationwide	●	●	●	●	●	●	●	●	●	●	●	●	●		Nationwide BS
Natwest	O	●	●	●	O	●	●	●	●	●	●	●	●	USA	Royal Bank of Scotland
Norwich & Peterborough	O	●	●	●	●	●	●	●	●	●	●	●	●		Norwich & Peterborough BS
Royal Bank of Scotland	O	●	●	●	O	●	●	●	●	●	●	●	●	USA	Royal Bank of Scotland
Woolwich	●	●	●	●	O	●	●	●	●	●	●	O	●	CON	Barclays Plc

Key

- ● Top rating (no criticisms found)
- O Middle rating
- ● Bottom rating
- ● A related company has a bottom rating and the company itself has a middle rating
- O A related company has a middle rating
- ● A related company has a bottom rating

Source: ECRA-See page 14 for full key to symbols.

THINK OF THE PLANET WHEN CHOOSING YOUR NEXT INVESTMENT

The Fund that looks after performance as well as the planet

Most of us would like to maximise returns from our investments, though not at the expense of the environment. Now, forward-looking companies also know that 'green' can spell out enhanced prospects and profits.

Spurred on by government targets and controls, such companies are developing cutting-edge technologies to meet new environmental standards – creating long-term investment opportunities in the process.

The **Jupiter Ecology Fund**, backed by the extensive resources of its own Environmental Research Unit, seeks out such companies across the world. Its approach has been fully vindicated by the returns achieved in the past – the Fund has been in the top 25% of all funds in the Global Growth sector over the last three years and five years.

Profit from Jupiter's 14 years of specialist ethical and environmental expertise.

For lump sum or regular investment, including your next ISA, talk to your financial adviser, call us free or visit the Jupiter website.

Past performance is no guarantee of future returns and the value of investments and the income from them can fall as well as rise.

FOR MORE INFORMATION CALL FREE ON
0500 0500 98
w w w . j u p i t e r o n l i n e . c o . u k

JUPITER

Leaders in long-term performance

Ethical Investment

One of the most effective ways you can put ethical consumerism into practice is with your investments. With the growth in awareness on the part of companies as well as investors of the benefits of ethical investment, it is becoming easier to put your money where your mouth is...

A LONG HISTORY

The roots of ethical investment can be traced to the religious movements of the nineteenth century, such as the Quakers and Methodists, whose concerns included issues such as temperance and fair employment conditions. At the beginning of the 1900s, the Methodist Church began investing in the stock market, consciously avoiding companies involved in alcohol and gambling.

During the twentieth century, more churches, charities and individuals began to take account of ethical criteria when making investment choices. An ethical investment ideology began to develop in the US as controversy over American involvement in the Vietnam War led to the founding of the Pax World Fund in 1971, which aimed to avoid investments associated with the war. In the 1980s, the apartheid regime in South Africa was the focal point for ethical investment and, indeed, its success as a tool of protest there accelerated its acceptance and growth round the world.

In 1983 the Ethical Investment Research Service (EIRIS) was established as the UK's first independent research service in ethical investment, providing the underlying research into companies' social, environmental and ethical performance needed by investors to make informed and socially responsible investment decisions. The UK's first ethically screened unit trust – the Stewardship Fund – was launched by Friends Provident a year later. Now there are over 60 ethical retail funds in the UK market, with an estimated value of £3.8 billion. This growth in SRI (socially responsible investment) has been reflected globally, for example the Asia-Pacific region has seen the launch of several SRI funds in places like Japan, Australia and Singapore. In Europe there were 170 ethical funds in 1999, by the end of 2001 the number had grown to over 280.

Ethical or socially responsible investment describes any area of the financial sector where the principles of the investor inform where they place their money. Companies large and small have an increasingly large impact upon the world around them. How they conduct their business can affect all manner of things

Ethical Investment sponsored by **JUPITER**
www.jupiteronline.co.uk   0500 050098

beyond the actual product or service they provide. There is a growing awareness that, alongside simply choosing to buy or not to buy their products, those of us who invest our spare money can also influence companies towards better social and environmental behaviour.

With any standard unit trust, investment trust, ISA or pension you may find your money going to companies which you would not wish to support. An ardent anti-smoker, for example would be dismayed to discover that their savings were invested in a tobacco company. Whether your investments are limited to a pension fund or if you're more involved in the stockmarket, knowing as much as you can about the ethics of the financial companies you're investing in can be as important as choosing an environmentally sound washing-up liquid. In fact, as the recent War on Want campaign to encourage the 10 million people who are occupational pension scheme members to find out where their money is invested shows, you can use your influence no matter how small your investments might seem.

HOW DO I BEGIN?

The first step towards positive investing is to identify what social, environmental and other ethical issues are most important to you. Areas of concern can be wide ranging, from animal testing to gambling, from human rights to nuclear power, from environmental enhancement to community involvement. Surveys by EIRIS have shown that the most prominent areas of concern were: operations in oppressive regimes,

THE GOOD SHOPPING GUIDE

The Good Shopping Guide is the world's first comprehensive ethical reference guide to clearly list the behaviour of the companies behind everyday consumer brands.

Our objective is to encourage a universally responsible corporate attitude to animal welfare, human rights and the environment.

Companies depend entirely on their customers' goodwill, so we believe that the key to a progressive 21st century lies in the persuasive power of intelligent consumer action.

breaking environmental regulations and testing products on animals. The companies that respondents most liked their pension fund to favour over others when making investments were those with good records on environmental issues and employment conditions. Identifying these areas will reflect the type of companies you want to invest in or to avoid.

NOBODY'S PERFECT

It is important, however, to remember that there is no such thing as a perfect company. All are involved in activities that someone somewhere will object to and none go far enough in terms of positive social and environmental contribution to satisfy all of the people all of the time. Ethical investment is about compromising and prioritising.

TYPES OF FUNDS

Once you've worked out your individual criteria, there are a diverse range of ethical funds available and different funds suit different investors. Some funds select a set of criteria which they believe will appeal to the widest range of investors. Others take a precisely focused approach, designed to appeal to a particular market. It is therefore very important to look behind the 'green' or 'ethical' label to what the fund is actually investing in before deciding to invest.

ASK:

- How the fund researches the activities of the companies in which it invests.
- Is there an ethical committee or advisory board that is independent of the investment process, to make sure the fund adheres to its published ethical policy?
- How good is the fund's communication with investors, e.g. does it have mechanisms in place to allow investors to voice their concerns?
- How active is the fund in engaging or communicating with companies? Does it encourage companies to improve their social and environmental performance?

THERE ARE THREE MAIN STRATEGIES THAT FUNDS CAN ADOPT TO IMPLEMENT THEIR ETHICAL INVESTMENT POLICIES.

- Engagement
  No companies are excluded but areas are identified in which companies can improve their environmental, social and ethical performance. The fund managers then 'engage' with the companies to encourage them to make such improvements.

- Preference
  The funds adopt social, environmental or other ethical guidelines which they prefer companies to meet. These guidelines are applied where all other things are equal (e.g. financial performance).

- Screening
  An 'acceptable list' of companies is created based on chosen positive and/or negative criteria (e.g. avoid companies involved in the arms trade, include companies with good environmental performance and so on). Funds are invested only in those companies on the list.

A TWO-PRONGED APPROACH

Ethical investing works two ways:
- by using their power as a shareholder to influence corporate behaviour;
- by choosing to invest only in companies who behave in a socially responsible manner

SHAREHOLDER POWER

One method of shareholder influence, which is as useful as much for the publicity it often receives, is the practice of posting shareholder resolutions which companies then have to consider in public at their annual general meetings. Campaigners say that the rules governing who can put forward a shareholder resolution are more restrictive in the UK than in the US. Nonetheless, a recent UK example is the resolution placed before BP's spring 2002 AGM – filed by the global environment network WWF, together with an international coalition of ethical investors – on its drilling activities in environmentally and culturally sensitive areas. This is one part of the campaign to prevent BP and others from drilling for oil in places such as the Alaskan Arctic National Wildlife Refuge, which is one of the last pristine areas left in the US and currently off-limits to oil and gas exploration and development.

VOTING FOR CHANGE

Shareholder resolutions, one of the more flamboyant ways of investing ethically, have been shown to work. Friends of the Earth used a shareholder resolution as part of its campaign against Balfour Beatty's plans to build a controversial dam in Turkey – the Ilisu dam on the Tiber River, 40 kilometres from the border of Syria and Iraq. Protest groups warned that the dam would make 78,000 local people homeless and drown dozens of towns and villages, including the world historic site of Hasankeyf.

FoE bought £30,000 worth of shares in order to submit a resolution on the dam contract at Balfour Beatty's AGM. Some months later, the company pulled out of the project, announcing that 'after a thorough evaluation of the commercial, environmental and social issues, it is not in the best interests of our stakeholders to pursue the project further.'

ALTERNATIVE INVESTMENT

Ethical investment is not confined to shares traded in stock exchanges. Many investors prefer to back individual projects or causes. Such directed investment is known by a variety of terms including, alternative investment, mission-based investment and socially directed investment. Examples of cause-based investment include regeneration projects in Birmingham (through the Aston Reinvestment Trust), and the support of projects in developing countries (through the co-operative lending society, Shared Interest). The cause-based investment sector is currently dominated by financial institutions such as Triodos Bank and the Ecology Building Society, although it also includes ethical companies who raise money directly from stakeholders by selling 'ethical shares'. Such companies include Traidcraft and the Centre for Alternative Technology.

Ethical Investment sponsored by **JUPITER**
www.jupiteronline.co.uk   0500 050098

GOOD FOR EVERYBODY

You don't need to worry that concentrating on ethical investments will make your financial performance suffer. Research by EIRIS and others indicates that investing according to ethical criteria may make little difference to overall financial performance, depending on the ethical policy applied. Five ethical indexes created by EIRIS produced financial returns roughly equivalent to the returns from the FTSE All-Share Index. For example, the total return of the Charities' Avoidance Index, which excludes the vast majority of companies involved in tobacco, gambling, alcohol, military sales and pornography, was 0.38 per cent greater than the All-Share.

And companies, too, can benefit. Over £3 billion is already invested in companies screened for good social, environmental and ethical practice by retail investors. Many churches and charities, pension schemes and local authorities are also investing according to socially responsible investment policies. That means money is being consciously diverted from companies that cannot demonstrate this good practice. And many investors are engaging with companies which they invest in or are considering investing in to persuade them to improve their policies and practices.

You can get further information by contacting the organisations listed below:

EIRIS's Guide to Ethical Funds covers the ethical retail funds (such as unit trusts, OEICs, investment trusts) available to the UK investor, giving a summary of each fund's ethical policy, top ten holdings and outlining what products (pension, ISA, etc.) are available with that fund.

A list of financial advisors who specialise in ethical investment is available from EIRIS's website: www.eiris.org, tel. 020 7840 5700)

The UK Social Investment Forum is a membership network that promotes and encourages socially responsible investment in the UK including shareholder activism, social banking and community finance, www.uksif.org tel. 020 7749 4880)

The European Sustainable and Responsible Investment Forum (Eurosif) is a non-profit organisation promoting the concept, practice and development of responsible and sustainable investment, www.eurosif.info

Below is a list of the ethical funds that *The Good Shopping Guide* was happy to publish and EIRIS was aware of at the time of collating this information and had been given details on by the fund provider. There may be other ethical funds that are on the market that EIRIS was not aware of or had no information on at that time. Note that by providing this list we are not making recommendations. For further information you may want to seek independent financial advice.

EIRIS defines an ethical fund as any fund which decides that shares are acceptable or not according to positive or negative ethical criteria e.g. environmental criteria, human rights criteria etc. The exception to this rule is that we do not include funds that only exclude companies involved in tobacco products.

AXA Sun Life Ethical Fund
Type of investment: OEIC
AXA Sun Life Fund Managers Ltd, MFD, PO Box 1810, Bristol BS99 5SN
Tel: 0117 989 0808
Fax: 0117 989 0604

Abbey Life Ethical Trust
Type of investment: Unit Trust
Abbey Life Investment Services Ltd, Abbey Life Centre, 100 Holdenhurst Road, Bournemouth BH8 8AL
Tel: 01202 292 373
Fax: 01202 292 403

Aberdeen Ethical World OEIC
Type of investment: OEIC
Address: Aberdeen Unit Trust Managers Ltd, One Bow Churchyard, Cheapside, London EC4M 9HH
Phone: 0845 300 2890
Fax: 020 7463 6507

Allchurches Amity Fund
Type of investment: OEIC
Address: Allchurches Investment Management Services Ltd, Beaufort House, Brunswick Road, Gloucester GL1 1JZ
Phone: 01452 305 958
Fax: 01452 311 690

Barchester Best of Green Life & Pension Funds, Barchester Best of Green Offshore
This fund also invests in the Jupiter Ecology Fund
Type of investment: Broker Fund
Address: Barchester Green Investment, Barchester House, 45 – 49 Catherine Street, Salisbury SP1 2DH
Phone: 01722 331 241
Fax: 01722 414191

CF Banner Real Life Unit Trust
Type of investment: Unit Trust
Address: Banner Financial Services, Banner House, Church Road, Copthorne, West Sussex RN10 3RA
Phone: 01342 717 917
Fax: 01342 712 534

CIS Environ Trust
Type of investment: Unit Trust
Address: CIS Unit Trust Managers Ltd, PO Box 105, Manchester M4 8BB
Phone: 0161 837 5060
Fax: 0161 837 4048

City Financial Ethical Fund
Type of investment: OEIC
Address: City Financial Investment Company Ltd, City Financial Centre, 88 Borough High Street, London SE1 1ST
Phone: 020 7556 8888
Fax: 020 7556 8889

Clerical Medical Ethical Fund
Type of investment: OEIC sub fund
Address: Clerical Medical Ethical Fund, Narrow Plain, Bristol BS2 0JH
Phone: 08457 772 233
Fax: 08457 772 234

Credit Suisse Fellowship Fund
Type of investment: OEIC
Address: Credit Suisse Asset Management Funds (UK) Ltd, Beaufort House, 15 St Botolph Street, London EC3A 7JJ
Phone: 020 7426 2929
Fax: 020 7426 2959

Ethical Investors Group Cruelty Free Funds
This fund is predominantly a fund of funds, ie it invests in other funds whose ethical policy may differ from that of this fund.
Continued on page 107

JUPITER sponsor Ethical Investment
www.jupiteronline.co.uk   0500 050098

Continued from page 105
Type of investment: Broker funds investing in other funds
and directly in equities
Address: Ethical Investors (UK) Ltd, Greenfield House,
Guiting Power, Cheltenham GL54 5TZ
Phone: 01451 850 777
Fax: 01451 850 705

**FIS UK ETHICAL TRUST (FIS), FP STEWARDSHIP FUNDS:
UNIT TRUST (SUT), INCOME TRUST (SIT), INTERNATIONAL
TRUST (SINT), LIFE FUND (SLF), MANAGED LIFE FUND
(SMLF), PENSION FUND (SPF), MANAGED PENSION FUND
(MPF)**
Type of investment: Unit trust (FIS, SUT, SIT, SINT), Life Fund
(SLF, SMLF), Pension Fund (SPF, MPF)
Address: 15 Old Bailey, London EC4M 7AP
Phone: 020 7506 1100
Fax: 020 7236 2060

FAMILY CHARITIES ETHICAL TRUST
Type of investment: Unit Trust
Address: 16 West St, Brighton BN1 2RE
Phone: 01273 725 272
Fax: 01273 206 026

FRAMLINGTON HEALTH FUND
Type of investment: Unit trust
Address: Framlington Unit Management Ltd, 155
Bishopsgate, London EC2M 3FT
Phone: 0845 777 5511
Fax: 020 7330 6638

HSBC AMANAH FUND
Type of investment: Fund based in Luxembourg
Address: 7 Rue du Marche-aux-Herbes, Luxembourg L-1728
Phone: 00 352 47 68 12 230
NB: These numbers are for dealing and administration;
marketing materials should be obtained from the local HSBC
Asset Management Representative

HALIFAX ETHICAL TRUST *
Type of investment: OEIC
Address: CMIM Retail Funds, 33 Old Broad Street, London
EC2N 1HZ
Phone: 01296 393 100
Fax: 020 7796 4824

HENDERSON ETHICAL FUND
Type of investment: OEIC
Address: Henderson Global Investors, 4 Broadgate, London
EC2M 2DA

Phone: 08457 832832
Fax: 020 7956 9191

HOMEOWNERS FRIENDLY SOCIETY FTSE4GOOD UK FUND
Type of investment: Single premium bond or savings plans
Address: Homeowners Friendly Society Ltd, Hornbeam
Avenue, Harrogate HG2 8XE
Phone: 0500 848 262
Fax: 01423 855 181

JUPITER ECOLOGY FUND
Type of investment: Unit Trust
Address: Jupiter Asset Management, 1 Grosvenor Place,
London SW1X 7JJ
Phone: 020 7412 0703
Fax: 020 7412 0705

JUPITER ENVIRONMENTAL OPPORTUNITIES FUND
Type of investment: Unit Trust
Address: Jupiter Asset Management, 1 Grosvenor Place,
London SW1X 7JJ
Phone: 020 7412 0703
Fax: 020 7412 0705

JUPITER GLOBAL GREEN INVESTMENT TRUST PLC
Type of investment: Investment Trust
Address: Jupiter Asset Management Ltd, PO Box 14470,
London SW1X 7YM
Phone: 0845 306 0100
Fax: n/a

LEGAL AND GENERAL ETHICAL TRUST
Type of investment: Unit Trust
Address: Legal and General Investments, Bucklersbury
House, 3 Queen Victoria Street, London EC4N 8NH
Phone: 020 7528 6200
Fax: 020 7528 6838

LINCOLN GREEN FUND
As well as investing directly in equities, this fund invests in
the Jupiter Ecology Fund.
Type of investment: Managed Life and Pension Funds
Address: Barnett Way, Barnwood, Gloucester GL4 3RZ
Phone: 01452 371 371
Fax: 01452 374 374

**MERCHANT INVESTORS ASSURANCE ETHICAL CAUTIOUS
MANAGED FUND ***
Type of investment: Managed Life and Pension Funds
Address: St Bartholomew's House, Lewins Mead, Bristol BS1
2NH
Phone: 0117 926 6366
Fax: 0117 975 2144

MINERVA GREEN PORTFOLIO AND MINERVA GREEN PROTECTOR PORTFOLIO
These are funds of funds, therefore the ethical policy is derived from those funds which Minerva invests in.
Type of investment: Unit Trust
Address: Minerva Fund Managers Ltd, Kelston View, Corston, Bath BA2 9AH
Phone: 01225 872 300
Fax: 01225 872 301

NPI GLOBAL CARE INCOME OEIC (INC), PENSION GLOBAL CARE MANAGED FUND (PMF)
Type of investment: OEIC (INC), Pension Fund (PMF),
Address: NPI House, 55 Calverly Road, Tunbridge Wells, Kent
Phone: 01892 515 151
Fax: n/a

NPI GLOBAL CARE GROWTH OEIC (GR), PENSION GLOBAL CARE (PF)
Type of investment: OEIC (GR), Pension Fund (PF),
Address: NPI House, 55 Calverly Road, Tunbridge Wells, Kent
Phone: 01892 515 151
Fax: n/a

NORWICH UNION UK ETHICAL FUND AND SUSTAINABLE FUTURE FUNDS (Corporate Bond, Managed, UK Growth, European Growth, Global Growth and Absolute Growth)
Type of investment: Unit Trust
Address: Norwich Union Investment Management, PO Box 4, Surrey Street, Norwich NR1 3NG
Phone: 01603 622 200
Fax: n/a

O M GERRARD ETHICAL FUND
Type of investment: Unit Trust
Address: The Registry, Royal Mint Court, London EC3N 4EY
Phone: 020 7709 4000
Fax: 020 7481 3798

SCOTTISH AMICABLE ETHICAL FUND
Type of investment: Unit Trust
Address: Scottish Amicable, Craigforth, PO Box 25, Stirling FK9 4UE
Phone: 01786 448 844
Fax: 01786 462 134

SCOTTISH EQUITABLE ETHICAL FUND
Scottish Equitable Socially Responsible Fund
Type of investment: OEIC
Address: Aegon Asset Management plc, Aegon House, 3 Lochside Avenue, Edinburgh Park, Edinburgh EH12 9SE
Phone: 0800 169 5196

Fax: 0131 549 4264

SCOTTISH LIFE UK ETHICAL FUND
Type of investment: Pension Fund
Address: Scottish Life Assurance Company, 19 St Andrew's Square, Edinburgh EH12 1YE
Phone: 0131 456 7777
Fax: 0131 456 7421

SCOTTISH WIDOWS ENVIRONMENTAL INVESTOR FUND *
Type of investment: Unit Trust
Address: Scottish Widows Unit Trust Managers Ltd, Charlton Place, Andover, Hants SP10 1RE
Phone: 0845 300 2244
Fax: n/a

SKANDIA ETHICAL PORTFOLIO
Type of investment: Managed life and pension fund
Address: Skandia Life, PO Box 37, Skandia House, Portland Terrace, Southampton SO14 7AY
Phone: 023 8033 4411
Fax: 023 8072 6637

SOVEREIGN ETHICAL FUND
Type of investment: Unit Trust
Address: Sovereign Unit Trust Managers Ltd, Tringham House, Wessex Fields, Deansleigh Road, Bournmouth BH7 7DT
Phone: 0800 731 1093
Fax: 01202 435 027

STANDARD LIFE UK ETHICAL FUND (SLUKF), STANDARD LIFE ETHICAL FUND (SLEF) and Standard Life Pension Ethical Fund (SLPEF)
Type of investment: OEIC (SLUKF), Life Fund (SLEF), Pension Fund (SLPEF)
Address: Standard Life Investment Company, 1 George Street, Edinburgh EH2 2LL (SLUKF)
Standard Life Assurance Company, 30 Lothian Road, Edinburgh EH1 2DH (SLEF, SLPEF)
Phone: 0800 333 353 (SLUKF) 0845 606 0100 (SLPEF, SLEF)
Fax: 0131 245 2390 (SLUKF) 0131 245 2429 (SLPEF, SLEF)

SUN LIFE GLOBAL PORTFOLIO ECOLOGICAL FUND
Type of investment: Off-shore fund
Address: Sun Life Global Management Ltd, Royalty House, Walpole Ave, Douglas, Isle of Man IM1 2SL
Phone: 01624 643 498
Fax: 01624 643 541

Good Food & Drink

Bottled water

The marketing of bottled water is largely hype but how else do we tell the difference between brands of a product that is colourless, odourless and largely tasteless? It's a business where the multinationals are in charge, even with brands like Malvern and Buxton. The worldwide market leaders are Evian, Volvic, Perrier and San Pellegrino, brands that are under the control of either Danone or Nestlé. (See the long table)

GLASS MOUNTAINS

Every bottle of Perrier sold around the world is bottled at source in Vergèze, France. So readers in say, Glasgow, would be drinking water that has travelled over 900 miles.

An environmental packaging solution is the re-usable glass bottle – like the milk bottle. In other European countries, higher proportions of all drinks come in returnable bottles. For example, in Germany, most mineral water is sold in a standard refillable glass bottle. The mineral water producers are members of a pool system, with their brands being distinguished by label but the bottles shared, allowing short transport distances from consumer to refiller. In the UK it seems that the big national breweries, soft drink producers and supermarkets are reluctant to use refillable glass bottles because of the extra effort (floor space and staff time) it would cause them. They prefer to encourage recycling, which hands the work over to the consumer, and they also much prefer dealing with plastics.

PURE, HOW PURE?

Although bottled water claims a natural, pure and healthy image, all waters must meet strict quality requirements. The area surrounding a Natural Mineral Water spring requires protection against pollution and although Natural Mineral Water is legally 'pure', this is not true of all water that is sold in bottles.

Those with high blood pressure, or others who need to follow a low sodium (salt) diet should check the mineral content of their water carefully. Natural mineral waters can only claim they're suitable for a low sodium diet if they contain less than 20mg per litre. Current advice from the Food Standards Agency is that some bottled waters shouldn't be used for babies. 'Waters to avoid are those with high levels of nitrate, nitrite, sodium, fluoride and sulphate. There are limits for these in tap, spring and other bottled drinking waters, but not in natural mineral waters.'

A *Health Which?* report concluded that in terms of bottled water, price varies considerably (from 12p/litre to £1.69/litre) and the quality is hardly ever proportional to the expense. To put this in context, the price of bottled water is on average 500 to 1,000 times higher than that of tap water.

ALTERNATIVES

The simplest course of action is to drink tap water. The Drinking Water Inspectorate has warned that if opportunities are not taken to improve the public perception of tap water, consumers would never appreciate the plentiful low cost water supplied to their taps. *Health Which?* echoed these sentiments by giving both filtered and unfiltered tap water from Thames Water a five out of five score in their taste test, a result which was only replicated by seven out of the 40 bottled water types in the report.

- 1180
- Aqua Pura
- Ballygowan
- Highland Spring
- Pennine Hills
- Spa
- Strathmore

- Campsie Spring
- Evian
- Volvic

- Malvern
- Perrier
- Vittel

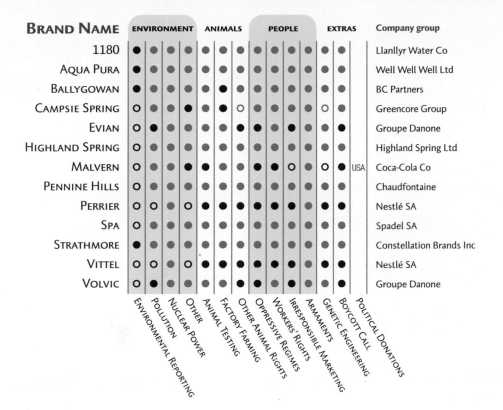

BRAND NAME	ENVIRONMENT	ANIMALS	PEOPLE	EXTRAS	Company group
1180					Llanllyr Water Co
AQUA PURA					Well Well Well Ltd
BALLYGOWAN					BC Partners
CAMPSIE SPRING					Greencore Group
EVIAN					Groupe Danone
HIGHLAND SPRING					Highland Spring Ltd
MALVERN				USA	Coca-Cola Co
PENNINE HILLS					Chaudfontaine
PERRIER					Nestlé SA
SPA					Spadel SA
STRATHMORE					Constellation Brands Inc
VITTEL					Nestlé SA
VOLVIC					Groupe Danone

Column headers (diagonal):
ENVIRONMENTAL REPORTING, POLLUTION, NUCLEAR POWER, OTHER, ANIMAL TESTING, FACTORY FARMING, OTHER ANIMAL RIGHTS, OPPRESSIVE REGIMES, WORKERS' RIGHTS, IRRESPONSIBLE MARKETING, ARMAMENTS, GENETIC ENGINEERING, BOYCOTT CALL, POLITICAL DONATIONS

Key

● Top rating (no criticisms found)

○ Middle rating

● Bottom rating

◐ A related company has a bottom rating and the company itself has a middle rating

○ A related company has a middle rating

● A related company has a bottom rating

Source: ECRA–See page 14 for full key to symbols.

113

Soft drinks

Kids just love fizzy drinks and most of us seem to be happy to buy it for them – but it's hardly a necessity of life! There's simply too much sugar, while ingredients like acids and caffeine are potentially harmful if taken in excess. We need to think about alternatives and, while we're at it, try to stop ourselves buying yet more plastic bottles that end up in the landfill.

SWEET AND DAMAGING

The average person consumes four pints of liquid each day. In the UK, around 20 per cent of this is in the form of soft drinks, with the volume slowly rising. High consumption of soft drinks means that other healthier drinks are being replaced. Apart from the water, there is very little in soft drinks that is even vaguely beneficial.

Whether still or fizzy, off-the-shelf soft drinks can contain the equivalent of up to 15 cubes of sugar, well over half the recommended daily maximum. This can lead to dental cavities and other health problems associated with high intakes of sugar. The acids in many soft drinks (found in both ordinary and no-sugar varieties) can also cause tooth decay and erosion of the hard enamel on the surface of the tooth and do not require the presence of plaque for this to occur. In 1996, research found that dental erosion as a result of drinking acidic drinks and other sources affected 30 per cent of 13-year-olds. Even Ribena's 'tooth-kind' drink failed dental tests carried out in two different studies.

All soft drinks given to children should be diluted to avoid tooth decay, given with meals if possible and in cups rather than bottles, as sipping drinks causes greater damage.

OTHER NASTIES

It's not just the sugar in soft drinks which can cause health problems. Caffeine, found in many fizzy drinks in varying levels, is addictive and can cause hyperactivity, disrupted sleep and withdrawal symptoms in children and adults. In Glasgow, a survey found an unusually high level of orofacial granulomatosis – an oral version of Crohn's disease which has been linked to a sensitivity to preservatives and flavourings in carbonated soft drinks. Research in the US has also found links between cola consumption and kidney stones in men. Artificial sweeteners – such as those found in many diet and no-sugar drinks – have also been linked with a number of health problems, although research has yet to prove any conclusive links.

115

CONFUSED IDENTITIES

At the time of research the following is the case: in the UK, Pepsi's brands are licensed to Britvic, which itself is owned by Bass plc. Consequently, Pepsi-owned brands receive the combined marks of Bass plc and Pepsico Inc (an amber circle on the table). Although the Libby's brand is no longer actually produced by Nestlé, it still owns the brand name. Hanover Acceptances subsidiary, Gerber Foods – the new licensee of the brand – has an agreement with Nestlé for the Libby's name, so consequently Baby Milk Action still lists Libby's in its Nestlé boycott information, because Nestlé still profits from it. This licensing agreement also applies to other ex-Nestlé brands, Um Bongo, Libby's C and Jusante. The Nestlé logo is now absent from all packaging, meaning that consumers may have unwittingly been buying Libby's brands believing them to be dissociated from the Nestlé empire. On the table, the Nestlé marks are those which are amber.

PACKAGING

Soft drinks are likely to come in aluminium or steel; glass; plastic bottles or cartons. The volume of packaging used each year is staggering. We use around six billion aluminium cans, 225 million plastic containers – mostly plastic bottles – and six billion glass containers annually. Less than a third of steel and aluminium cans and only five per cent of plastics are recycled in the UK, the remainder being landfilled or incinerated. Glass is the best option, as it can be recycled indefinitely.

KEEPING HEALTHY - AND GREEN

- One soft drink in a day has usually more than an enough extra energy for one person
- Use glass bottles not plastic ones
- Recycle plastic bottles
- If you buy cans, make sure you crunch and recycle them

- Irn Bru
- Rio
- Rubicon
- Vimto
- Whole Earth

- Aqua Libra
- Britvic
- Purdey's
- Robinsons
- Virgin Cola

- Coca-Cola
- Libby's
- Pepsi
- Schweppes
- Sunny Delight
- Ribena

Brand Name	Environment				Animals			People				Extras				Company group
	Environmental Reporting	Pollution	Nuclear Power	Other	Animal Testing	Factory Farming	Other Animal Rights	Oppressive Regimes	Workers' Rights	Irresponsible Marketing	Armaments	Genetic Engineering	Boycott Call	Political Donations		
Aqua Libra														CON		Six Continents
Britvic														CON		Six Continents
Coca-Cola														USA		Coca Cola Co Inc
Irn Bru																AG Barr Plc
Libby's																Hanover Acceptances/Nestle
Pepsi														CON		Pepsico/Six Continents
Purdey's														CON		Six Continents
Ribena														USA		Glaxo Smithkline
Rio														CON		Hall & Woodhouse
Robinsons														CON		Six Continents
Rubicon																Rubicon Products
Schweppes														USA		Coca Cola Co Inc
Sunny Delight																Procter & Gamble
Whole Earth																Whole Earth Foods
Vimto																Nichols Plc
Virgin Cola														LAB		Virgin Group of Companies

Key

- ● Top rating (no criticisms found)
- ○ Middle rating
- ● Bottom rating
- ◐ A related company has a bottom rating and the company itself has a middle rating
- ○ A related company has a middle rating
- ● A related company has a bottom rating

Source: ECRA-See page 14 for full key to symbols.

Tea & Coffee

Tea and coffee were the first products used to spearhead the 'fair trade' campaign for a better deal for Third World farmers and plantation workers. Now, after years of perseverance, the campaign has begun to score real success, especially with most of the supermarket groups taking the issues of socially-responsible sourcing seriously. The public have caught on too – at least one in five people now recognise the Fairtrade mark and know that it signifies a better deal for Third World producers. The key point they recognise is that more of the selling price goes to the producers and therefore less goes to the traders and big corporations.

FAIR TRADING

The world of tea and coffee is beginning to show us how the more ethical markets of the future will evolve, but consumer vigilance will always be vital to maintain and improve upon the gains. Some of the big food companies are still peddling false claims about the fair trading of their goods when it is clear that they do nothing of the sort. The Fairtrade Foundation's website (*www.fairtrade.org.uk*) keeps up to date with the latest developments.

The key criteria that decide whether a brand deserves the Fairtrade Mark are usually the following: collective bargaining and representation for workers; good basic wages or purchase prices; welfare provisions; health and safety; environmental practices; and long-term trading relationships based on continuity and mutual advantage.

cafédirect° sponsors Tea & Coffee

www.cafedirect.co.uk

SOCIAL CONDITIONS

Wages and conditions for tea plantation workers are often poor, with their living facilities below acceptable standards. It is hoped that the fair trade campaign will have a long-term beneficial effect on these.

As coffee is often grown by independent farmers, the everyday problems are more to do with the price they receive for their crop and the frequent delays they suffer in receiving payments. Again, the fair trade campaign is trying to address these procedural difficulties, although these are often a symptom of the overall economic or political conditions of the countries where the crop is grown.

ENVIRONMENT

In the tea plantations, pesticides are often mixed in the fields without proper dedicated drainage and treatment. Workers say that protective masks, goggles or gloves are rarely provided. The same is true of the large coffee plantations in Brazil and Colombia, where the cultivation is also so intensive that natural nutrients are drained away and have to be replaced with fertilisers. In the long term, it is hoped that workers and farmers will become more aware of the dangers and hazards and that the plantation companies will adopt more responsible policies.

BRANDS ON THE SHELVES

Amongst the fairly-traded tea brands are Clipper's, Equal Exchange, Hampstead, Ridgways, Themis, Traidcraft and Teadirect.

The fairly-traded coffee brands include Cafédirect, Brian Wogan's, Co-op Fair Trade, Equal Exchange, Johnsons Fairtrade, Matthew Algie's, Percol, Sainsbury's Fairtrade and Traidcraft.

The quality and range of this sector is getting better and better – for example Cafédirect now do an excellent organic variety and Teadirect now also do a delicious organic green tea.

Excellent
cafédirect°
from the growers

5065

THE HEIGHT OF COFFEE TASTE

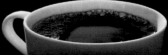

www.cafedirect.co.uk

Tea & Coffee is sponsored by cafédirect®

www.cafedirect.co.uk

TEA

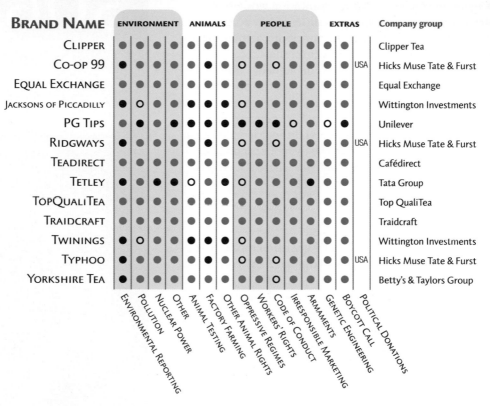

Brand Name	Environment				Animals			People					Extras			Company group
	Environmental Reporting	Pollution	Nuclear Power	Other	Animal Testing	Factory Farming	Other Animal Rights	Oppressive Regimes	Workers' Rights	Code of Conduct	Irresponsible Marketing	Armaments	Genetic Engineering	Boycott Call	Political Donations	
Clipper	●	●	●	●	●	●	●	●	●	●	●	●	●	●		Clipper Tea
Co-op 99	●	●	●	●	●	●	●	○	●	○	●	●	●	●	USA	Hicks Muse Tate & Furst
Equal Exchange	●	●	●	●	●	●	●	●	●	●	●	●	●	●		Equal Exchange
Jacksons of Piccadilly	●	○	●	●	●	●	●	○	●	●	●	●	●	●		Wittington Investments
PG Tips	●	●	●	●	●	●	●	●	●	●	○	●	○	●		Unilever
Ridgways	●	●	●	●	●	●	●	○	●	○	●	●	●	●	USA	Hicks Muse Tate & Furst
Teadirect	●	●	●	●	●	●	●	●	●	●	●	●	●	●		Cafédirect
Tetley	●	●	●	●	○	●	●	○	●	●	●	●	●	●		Tata Group
TopQualiTea	●	●	●	●	●	●	●	●	●	●	●	●	●	●		Top QualiTea
Traidcraft	●	●	●	●	●	●	●	●	●	●	●	●	●	●		Traidcraft
Twinings	●	○	●	●	●	●	●	○	●	●	●	●	●	●		Wittington Investments
Typhoo	●	●	●	●	●	●	●	○	●	○	●	●	●	●	USA	Hicks Muse Tate & Furst
Yorkshire Tea	●	●	●	●	●	●	●	●	○	●	●	●	●	●		Betty's & Taylors Group

GOOD SHOPPING GUIDE 2003 ETHICAL

- Clipper
- Equal Exchange
- Teadirect
- TopQualiTea
- Traidcraft

?

- Co-op 99
- Ridgways
- Typhoo
- Yorkshire Tea

- Jacksons of Piccadilly
- PG Tips
- Tetley
- Twinings

COFFEE

BRAND NAME	ENVIRONMENT				ANIMALS			PEOPLE					EXTRAS			Company group
	Environmental Reporting	Pollution	Nuclear Power	Other	Animal Testing	Factory Farming	Other Animal Rights	Oppressive Regimes	Workers' Rights	Code of Conduct	Irresponsible Marketing	Armaments	Genetic Engineering	Boycott Call	Political Donations	
CAFÉDIRECT	●	●	●	●	●	●	●	●	●	●	●	●	●	●		Cafédirect
CARTE NOIR	○	○	●	●	●	●	●	●	●	●	●	●	○	●	USA	Philip Morris
DOUWE EGBERTS	○	●	●	●	●	●	●	●	●	●	●	●	●	●		Sara Lee Corp
EQUAL EXCHANGE	●	●	●	●	●	●	●	●	●	●	●	●	●	●		Equal Exchange
KENCO	○	○	●	●	●	●	●	●	●	●	●	●	○	●	USA	Philip Morris
LAVAZZA	●	●	●	●	●	●	●	●	●	●	●	●	●	●		Luigi Lavazza SpA
MAXWELL HOUSE	○	○	●	●	●	●	●	●	●	●	●	●	○	●	USA	Philip Morris
NESCAFE	○	○	●	○	●	●	●	●	●	●	●	●	●	●		Nestlé
PERCOL	●	●	●	●	●	●	●	●	●	●	●	●	●	●		Food Brands Group
ROMBOUTS	●	●	○	●	●	○	●	○	●	●	●	●	○	●		Doughty-Hanson
TRAIDCRAFT	●	●	●	●	●	●	●	●	●	●	●	●	●	●		Traidcraft

Key

- ● Top rating (no criticisms found)
- ○ Middle rating
- ● Bottom rating
- ● A related company has a bottom rating and the company itself has a middle rating
- ○ A related company has a middle rating
- ● A related company has a bottom rating

Source: ECRA-See page 14 for full key to symbols.

GOOD SHOPPING GUIDE 2003 ETHICAL

- Cafédirect
- Equal Exchange
- Percol
- Traidcraft

- Douwe Egberts
- Lavazza
- Rombouts

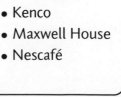

- Carte Noir
- Kenco
- Maxwell House
- Nescafé

Beer, lager & cider

The big brewers may all be thinking globally these days but seasoned drinkers usually prefer their local brews when they can find them. Where the big companies often win is by persuading us that a 'local' brew from far away contains something special or unique – hence the successes of brews from Mexico, South Africa, India and Thailand.

Below we cover the big companies with nationwide brands of bitter, lager, stout or cider. The table indicates the ownership of the draught brands – which may not be the same as that of bottles and cans of the same brand.

HOW MANY MILES

Our increasingly exotic tastes could be causing horrendous and fairly pointless pollution of the globe. Ingredients for a real ale from a local brewery might have travelled about 600 miles in all, which might seem far enough, but for some imported lagers produced by the multinationals the ingredients can travel as many as 24,000 miles. There may be some consolation in the fact that many of the so-called 'export' or 'continental' lagers are really brewed under licence in the UK, but there is ever more beer moving across European borders these days.

WHAT'S IN THE STUFF?

Conventional hop farming uses a lot of pesticides – which results in what the pressure group Sustain describes as 'scorched earth' farming methods, where the ground between and beneath the hops is kept barren and dusty. Organic farming methods use mustard mixed with the hops to attract predators and combat aphid attacks.

Traditionally, the barley for malting has come from the highest-quality spring crops but recently there has been massive development of new winter barley varieties, on which farmers use almost double the number of pesticides. These changes, and the decrease in planting of summer barley, have badly damaged bird populations.

Under current UK legislation, drinks containing over 1.2 per cent alcohol are exempt from the compulsory labelling applicable to other products for consumption. This means that brewers don't tell us when they use chemical additives, as many do to increase the shelf life of the beer or to alter the colour or flavour of the brew. The lack of mandatory labelling causes problems for vegetarians, as most beers do still use animal-derived products.

ORGANIC OPTIONS

Organic beers have begun to take off although there are real problems finding organic hops – the main source of supply being far-off New Zealand! Organic production of hops in the UK is not only possible but potentially highly profitable.

Brewing your own beer can potentially give you control over many elements of the brewing process. There are no UK homebrew suppliers currently stocking organic hops, however, these are available by mail order from the US (*www.Seven-bridges-cooperative.com*). While this increases beer miles, the weight of the product is only around 3lbs. Online brewing classes are now available on the web (*www.breworganic.com/index.htm*) with lots of the information you need, from the best equipment to bottling the finished product.

ONE FOR THE ROAD

The legal driving alcohol limit in the UK is 80mg%, compared with 50mg% in most of Europe and 20mg% in Sweden.

Although any alcohol affects all drivers, accident rates for young people double after only two drinks and increase tenfold after five drinks.

BASIC DRINKING ETHICS

Don't let ethics spoil your fun...
- ....but you really should never drink then drive
- Try to support the local pubs that stock local brews
- Cans are best for drinking outdoors – and bottles are best at home
- When drinking out anywhere, always remove your empties

- Dry Blackthorn
- Holsten Pils
- Marston's
- Merrydown
- Old Speckled Hen
- Strongbow
- Wadworth's 6x

- Carling
- ESB
- Fosters
- Guinness
- John Smiths

- Beck's
- Budweiser
- Carlsberg
- Grolsch
- Heineken
- Miller
- Stella Artois

BRAND NAME	ENVIRONMENT				ANIMALS			PEOPLE				EXTRAS			Company group
	Environmental Reporting	Pollution	Nuclear Power	Other	Animal Testing	Factory Farming	Other Animal Rights	Oppressive Regimes	Workers' Rights	Irresponsible Marketing	Armaments	Genetic Engineering	Boycott Call	Political Donations	
BEER & LAGER															
Beck's															Interbrew
Budweiser														USA	Anheuser-Busch
Carling														USA	Adolph Coors Company
Carlsberg															Carlsberg AS/Orkla AS
ESB														CON	Fuller, Smith & Turner
Fosters														CON	Scottish & Newcastle Plc/Fosters group Ltd
Grolsch														USA	Adolph Coors Company/Koninklijke Grolsch NV
Guinness															Diageo Plc
Heineken															Whitbread/Heineken NV
Holsten Pils															Holsten Brauerei AG
John Smiths														CON	Scottish & Newcastle Plc
Marston's															Wolverhampton & Dudley
Miller														CON	Scottish & Newcastle Plc/Phillip Morris
Old Speckled Hen															Greene King
Stella Artois															Interbrew
Wadworth's 6X															Wadworth & Co
CIDER															
Dry Blackthorn															Constellation Brands
Strongbow															HP Bulmers Ltd
Merrydown															Merrydown Plc

Key

- ● Top rating (no criticisms found)
- ○ Middle rating
- ● Bottom rating
- ◑ A related company has a bottom rating and the company itself has a middle rating
- ○ A related company has a middle rating
- ● A related company has a bottom rating

Source: ECRA-See page 14 for full key to symbols.

125

Bananas

Although British consumers have always loved bananas, it is only recently that we have really begun to notice the different kinds available or where they actually come from. As with many farmed products from tropical countries there is now a strong move towards fair trade bananas. Bananas are important in the fair trade campaign because of the threat from big plantation companies to the livelihoods of people living in the Windward islands of the Caribbean where bananas often provide the only reliable employment. There are other issues to think about as well, especially the heavy use of pesticides, and there is now a campaign for organic methods of growing the fruit.

BANANA WARS

The US and the EU went through a long dispute about the trading conditions for bananas during the 90s. The European countries tried to keep preferential access for bananas from the Caribbean islands, but the World Trade Organisation eventually ruled in favour of the US. This means that the 'dollar banana companies' like Chiquita, Dole and Del Monte have been able to expand their business in Europe. European companies like Fyffes and Geest import their fruit mainly, but not exclusively, from the Windward islands.

Windward bananas are grown much less intensively and more sustainably than those from other countries, especially those in Central America. Most production is done by small producers with better employment conditions and with fewer chemicals than elsewhere. Windward bananas also tend to be smaller and sweeter.

WAGES & CONDITIONS

The big multinationals operating in Central and South America own sprawling plantations where workers may toil for 12 hours a day in poor conditions, as well as face intimidation by owners. Workers have been trying to organise trade unions to bargain for better wages and conditions but have encountered company harassment, especially in Costa Rica and Honduras.

A good way for us to influence the way workers are treated in these countries is to opt for fair trade bananas which, after some delay, have been accepted by a number of supermarket chains in Britain.

PESTICIDES & CHEMICALS

Since the 1960s companies increasingly have been growing varieties of bananas with the highest yields. These are, however, also very susceptible to pests and diseases and so the industry uses an enormous quantity of chemicals throughout the growing process, before and after harvesting, as well as to preserve the fruit in transit. While the average usage of pesticides on farms in industrialised countries is 2.7kg per hectare, within the Costa Rican banana industry the figure is 44kg per hectare, with aerial spraying occurring up to 50 times a year. The workers are exposed to appalling health hazards and the surrounding areas can become seriously contaminated.

ORGANIC OPTIONS

Planting varieties of bananas that are more resistant to infection is the most obvious way of reducing the justification for such heavy use of pesticides. Increasing numbers of bananas are being imported from farms where they are grown without chemical assistance. This market is sure to increase as customers become more aware of the issues and observant of the different brands available.

- Fyffes
- Geest

- Del Monte
- Dole

- Chiquita

BANANAS

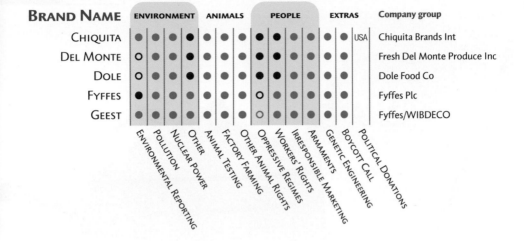

BRAND NAME	ENVIRONMENT				ANIMALS			PEOPLE				EXTRAS			Company group
	Environmental Reporting	Pollution	Nuclear Power	Other	Animal Testing	Factory Farming	Other Animal Rights	Oppressive Regimes	Workers' Rights	Irresponsible Marketing	Armaments	Genetic Engineering	Boycott Call	Political Donations	
CHIQUITA													USA		Chiquita Brands Int
DEL MONTE															Fresh Del Monte Produce Inc
DOLE															Dole Food Co
FYFFES															Fyffes Plc
GEEST															Fyffes/WIBDECO

Key

- ● Top rating (no criticisms found)
- ○ Middle rating
- ● Bottom rating
- ◕ A related company has a bottom rating and the company itself has a middle rating
- ◯ A related company has a middle rating
- ● A related company has a bottom rating

Source: ECRA-See page 14 for full key to symbols.

The new gold standard for chocolate

Every time you take a bite of delicious Divine chocolate you can be sure the Ghanaian cocoa growers were paid fairly for their cocoa beans so they can have better lives and share in your enjoyment

www.divinechocolate.com

Chocolate bars

It may not come as a surprise that the British public are among the highest per capita consumers of chocolate in the world. The average person here eats the equivalent of 180 bars of Dairy Milk a year and – this is more difficult to believe – eats more chocolate than fruit and vegetables combined! Whether or not we are chocoholics ourselves, the key issues to consider are the health factors for consumers, the environmental issues and whether cocoa farmers are getting a fair deal from the chocolate manufacturers. Here we look at the chocolate snack bars like Mars Bars, Kit Kats and Snickers, which are especially high in fat and sugar, rather than the biscuit bars like Penguins or the large chocolate-only bars.

INSTANT SATISFACTION

Chocolate snacks are attractive and satisfying. They keep hunger at bay, the sugar helps to boost energy levels and the chocolate coating guarantees their irresistibility, but in reality these snacks have little nutritional value. The average bar contains around 25g of sugar, and yet it is well known that excess sugar consumption may lead to obesity, tooth decay and diabetes. Clearly a much healthier alternative would be to eat cereal bars or fruit.

Some plain chocolate snack bars contain unnecessary milk derivatives, making them unsuitable for vegans. There is also scientific concern about the survival of pesticide residues in chocolate throughout the manufacturing process.

ENVIRONMENTAL ISSUES

Cocoa beans are heavily sprayed with numerous pesticides to try to defeat the endemic infestations and diseases that attack the crop in Africa and Latin America. The heavy use of pesticides can have damaging health effects on cocoa workers who may not be provided with protective clothing or safety training. Conventional cocoa plantations also destroy natural habitats. Organic plantations can, however, sustain the rain forest very effectively. Recently, organic chocolate has at last begun to catch on with consumers.

FAIR TRADE

Cocoa is big business and one that is heavily dominated by multinational manufacturing and trading companies.

The multinationals subcontract the buying to traders who make their own profits, leaving the small farmers at the bottom end of the trade. This means that the cocoa farmers in West Africa and Latin America never get to share in the profits of the business, not least because the cocoa prices paid to them bear no relation to the cost of chocolate bars to consumers in the industrialised countries. Cocoa prices, which are set in the financial centres of New York and London, fluctuate wildly, making it hard for the growing countries to get past first base in the development of the industry.

The fair trade campaign hopes to ensure that the prices paid for cocoa beans are more stable and it aims to give organisations direct access to the cocoa market and to encourage farmers to operate independently of intermediary traders.

Many of the companies approached during our research failed to provide information about their Codes of Conduct with regard to Cocoa growers. Although Cadbury's did provide a document entitled Codes of Conduct with some good points in it, it did not refer specifically to workers' rights at supplier companies, for example. Fairly traded brands include Divine, Dubble, Traidcraft, Maya Gold and Green & Black's.

For more information on how the codes of conduct are rated on the long table see the relevent category definition in the introduction.

- Divine
- Dubble
- Green and Black's
- Maya Gold
- Ritter Sport
- Thornton's

- Dairy Milk
- Fry's

- Chocolate Orange
- Galaxy
- Kit Kat
- Mars Bar

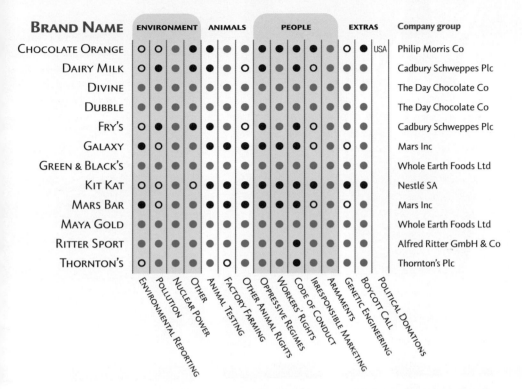

Brand Name	ENVIRONMENT				ANIMALS			PEOPLE					EXTRAS			Company group

Column headers (left to right): Environmental Reporting, Pollution, Nuclear Power, Other, Animal Testing, Factory Farming, Other Animal Rights, Oppressive Regimes, Workers' Rights, Code of Conduct, Irresponsible Marketing, Armaments, Genetic Engineering, Boycott Call, Political Donations

Brand Name / Company group:
- Chocolate Orange — Philip Morris Co (USA)
- Dairy Milk — Cadbury Schweppes Plc
- Divine — The Day Chocolate Co
- Dubble — The Day Chocolate Co
- Fry's — Cadbury Schweppes Plc
- Galaxy — Mars Inc
- Green & Black's — Whole Earth Foods Ltd
- Kit Kat — Nestlé SA
- Mars Bar — Mars Inc
- Maya Gold — Whole Earth Foods Ltd
- Ritter Sport — Alfred Ritter GmbH & Co
- Thornton's — Thornton's Plc

Key

- ● Top rating (no criticisms found)
- ○ Middle rating
- ● Bottom rating
- ● A related company has a bottom rating and the company itself has a middle rating
- ○ A related company has a middle rating
- ● A related company has a bottom rating

Source: ECRA-See page 14 for full key to symbols.

Potato crisps

We hardly need telling that the most inviting and innocent-looking packet of crisps is more about clever marketing than good food, but we should also be aware of the hidden dangers. The manufacturers fall over themselves to make kids love crisps but they are also very good at keeping quiet about the additives they put in. These commonly include monosodium glutamate (MSG) and saccharin, ingredients that are banned, for good reasons, in foods for babies and young children.

PUTTING ON WEIGHT

Crisps were pioneered in the 1920s by Smiths, which is these days part of Pepsico, as is Walkers, so that Pepsico now has more than 37 per cent of the market. The second largest share of 12 per cent is held by United Biscuits, which owns McVities and KP. Golden Wonder has about 5 per cent of the market. On the plus side of this big company domination, at least we can take some comfort from the fact that most crisps eaten in the UK are also produced here.

As the crisp market has long been at or near saturation point, companies have been trying to get us to eat more by increasing the pack size to American proportions, where monster packs are normal. There has also been growing competition to traditional potato crisps from snacks like Pringles, which are extruded from a mix of ingredients, and tortilla chips, which are based on maize, one of the major GM crops.

ORGANIC & VEGETARIAN

At the time of this survey (June 1999), the organic crisps available included Tra'fo and Apache, which were clearly GM-free. The manufacturer of Apache was known to test for cross-contamination with GM crops. The only vegetable oils used in preparation that could be identified as GM-free were sunflower or peanut oil. There was a risk that other oils might contain soya from non-segregated crops. There was also a number of additives that could come from GM crops, including E322 (lecithin), E471 (which could be made from soya oil) and E621 (monosodium glutamate, made from fermentation of vegetable protein such as soya.

Both MSG and saccharin are commonly found in crisps. MSG may cause 'Chinese restaurant syndrome', including headaches, palpitations and dizziness. Saccharin may be linked to cancer. The preservatives E260 and E262 have also been linked to cancers.

Companies that said that all flavours were suitable for vegetarians were Jacobs

(Twiglets), Terra Prima (Apache), Jonathan Crisp, and Faan Zuidhorn. Lactose or 'milk proteins' are often added to crisps, making them unsuitable for vegans.

PACKAGING

Crisp packaging keeps getting fancier, with laminated foil packs replacing polypropylene, and with some ridiculously elaborate composite boxes. At the time of research, Pringles carton contained six different materials, including steel, aluminium, PET and polyethylene plastics. In such composite form, recycling is difficult or impossible.

- Apache Tortillas
- Jonathan Crisp
- Jordans
- Kettle Chips

- Bensons
- Golden Wonder
- Seabrook Crisps

- KP
- Phileas Fogg
- Pringles
- Smiths
- Twiglets
- Walkers

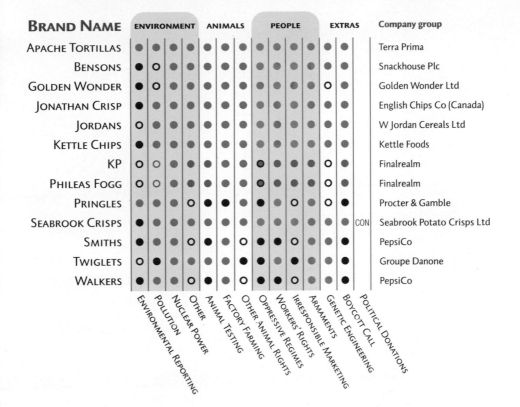

BRAND NAME	ENVIRONMENT	ANIMALS	PEOPLE	EXTRAS	Company group
APACHE TORTILLAS					Terra Prima
BENSONS					Snackhouse Plc
GOLDEN WONDER					Golden Wonder Ltd
JONATHAN CRISP					English Chips Co (Canada)
JORDANS					W Jordan Cereals Ltd
KETTLE CHIPS					Kettle Foods
KP					Finalrealm
PHILEAS FOGG					Finalrealm
PRINGLES					Procter & Gamble
SEABROOK CRISPS				CON	Seabrook Potato Crisps Ltd
SMITHS					PepsiCo
TWIGLETS					Groupe Danone
WALKERS					PepsiCo

Column headers (left to right):
ENVIRONMENTAL REPORTING, POLLUTION, NUCLEAR POWER, OTHER, ANIMAL TESTING, FACTORY FARMING, OTHER ANIMAL RIGHTS, OPPRESSIVE REGIMES, WORKERS' RIGHTS, IRRESPONSIBLE MARKETING, ARMAMENTS, GENETIC ENGINEERING, BOYCOTT CALL, POLITICAL DONATIONS

Key

● Top rating (no criticisms found)

○ Middle rating

● Bottom rating

◗ A related company has a bottom rating and the company itself has a middle rating

◔ A related company has a middle rating

◑ A related company has a bottom rating

Source: ECRA-See page 14 for full key to symbols.

Biscuits

Children's biscuits and so-called 'healthy' biscuits are two of the fastest-growing sectors in an already saturated food market. The whole idea is hardly a healthy one – a biscuit is just a sugary, fatty treat to be enjoyed, hopefully in moderation. Meanwhile the companies make confusing claims that their biscuits are '85 per cent fat free'. Consumers tend to think these have less fat than 'low fat' ones when they have just as much as an average slice of cheesecake. Surveys have shown that more than half of consumers have no idea what these labels actually mean. The companies are happy as long as they're persuading us their bikkies are good, OK, healthy – whatever, just as long as we buy them.

CORPORATE CRUNCH-UP

At the time of research, the biscuit market was a perfect example of global corporate crunching. A lowly Somerfield 'basics' digestive was made by McVities – which is owned by United Biscuits, which is owned by Finalrealm, which is a consortium of Nabisco, DB Capital, Cinven and PAI. Of those in the consortium, Nabisco is owned by Kraft, which is owned by Philip Morris, the company that makes Marlboro cigarettes but has changed its name to Altria. Cinven is a leverage buy-out operation which owns companies as diverse as Odeon Cinemas, Foesco chemicals and William Hill Bookmakers. DB Capital Partners is owned by Deutsche Bank, which has been involved in financing controversial dams amongst other things. So what's new?

INGREDIENTS

Vegetarians and vegans should be aware that many biscuits contain dairy products such as butter or whey powders. Some brands may contain non-specific animal fat. Companies are realising that consumers do often look at the labels. In the mid-1990s, Greenpeace famously persuaded McVities to stop making biscuits with fish oil from industrial fishing.

One biscuit-maker, Northern Foods, says that none of its biscuits are tainted with GM because consumers won't buy GM food. That's fine, but we should be aware that the powerful food industry lobby, the Food and Drink Federation, states: 'Biotechnology, including genetic modification, offers enormous potential to improve the quality and quantity of the food supply.' In the US, Kraft has been using untested and unlabelled genetically engineered ingredients for several years, although in Europe the company has so far been respectful of consumer pressure. Now, more than ever, is a time for vigilance against the stealthy introduction of GM technology. Try to buy Walkers, Traidcraft, Doves Farm or Bahlsen

- Bahlsen
- Doves Farm
- Traidcraft
- Walkers

- Burton's
- Fox's
- Hill

- Jacobs
- McVities

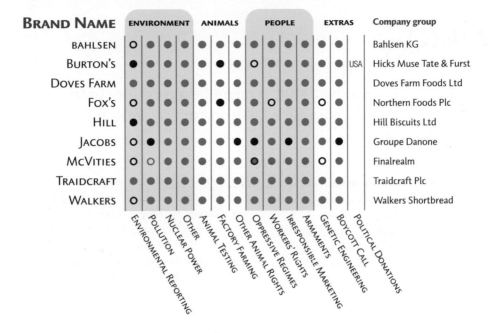

Brand Name	Environment				Animals			People				Extras			Company group
	Environmental Reporting	Pollution	Nuclear Power	Other	Animal Testing	Factory Farming	Other Animal Rights	Oppressive Regimes	Workers' Rights	Irresponsible Marketing	Armaments	Genetic Engineering	Boycott Call	Political Donations	
BAHLSEN	○	●	●	●	●	●	●	●	●	●	●	●	●	●	Bahlsen KG
BURTON'S	●	●	●	●	●	●	●	○	●	●	●	●	●	● USA	Hicks Muse Tate & Furst
DOVES FARM	●	●	●	●	●	●	●	●	●	●	●	●	●	●	Doves Farm Foods Ltd
FOX'S	○	●	●	●	●	●	●	●	○	●	●	○	●	●	Northern Foods Plc
HILL	●	●	●	●	●	●	●	●	●	●	●	●	●	●	Hill Biscuits Ltd
JACOBS	○	●	●	●	●	●	●	●	●	●	●	●	●	●	Groupe Danone
McVITIES	○	○	●	●	●	●	●	●	●	●	●	●	○	●	Finalrealm
TRAIDCRAFT	●	●	●	●	●	●	●	●	●	●	●	●	●	●	Traidcraft Plc
WALKERS	○	●	●	●	●	●	●	●	●	●	●	●	●	●	Walkers Shortbread

Key

- ● Top rating (no criticisms found)
- ○ Middle rating
- ● Bottom rating
- ◉ A related company has a bottom rating and the company itself has a middle rating
- ○ A related company has a middle rating
- ● A related company has a bottom rating

Source: ECRA-See page 14 for full key to symbols.

Whisky

Before we start on 'the hard stuff' it might be a good idea to try and get a few things straight, because once we're on our way we're sure to forget!

WHAT'S IN IT?

The name whisky comes from Irish Gaelic *usque baugh*, or Scottish Gaelic *uisge beatha*, meaning 'water of life'.

For no good reason, the spirit distilled in Scotland and Canada is spelt 'whisky' while in Ireland and America they spell it 'whiskey'. Wherever it's from, the stuff is distilled from the fermented mash of cereal grains. In Scotland the main grain used is barley. In Ireland, other grains may be used with barley. In Canada and America, the grains are usually rye and maize (the latter is known over there simply as 'corn').

Things distinguishing the flavour include the quality of the water, the drying of the grain (in many Scottish distilleries this is done over peat fires) and the oak casks in which the spirit is matured.

DIFFERENT KINDS

- 'Blended' whisky, which is the most commonly drunk in Britain, can be a combination of up to 50 different malt and grain whiskies.
- 'Malt' whisky is made from malted (or sprouted) grains. A whisky simply labelled as 'malt' may include malt whiskies from several different distilleries.

- To be labelled 'single malt', a whisky has to come from only one distillery.
- 'Grain' whisky is made from a mixture of malted barley and unmalted grains such as wheat or maize.
- Irish whiskey is distilled three times rather than twice, which is usual for Scotch, and is made from malted and unmalted barley as well as other grains such as maize.

The best overall scoring brands are Glenmorangie, owned by Glenmorangie Plc, and Grants, who are owned by William Grant and Sons. Next comes Famous Grouse, Jameson and Whyte & Mackay. Bells and Teachers fall into the lowest section of this relatively high scoring product category. Which ones taste best is up to you!

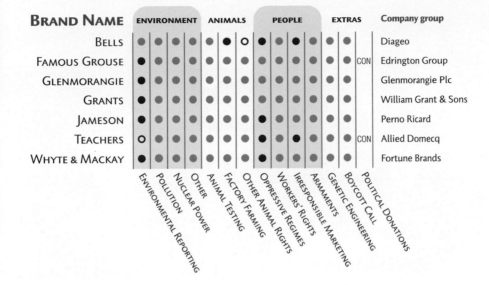

BRAND NAME	ENVIRONMENT				ANIMALS			PEOPLE				EXTRAS			Company group
BELLS	●	●	●	●	●	●	○	●	●	●	●	●	●		Diageo
FAMOUS GROUSE	●	●	●	●	●	●	●	●	●	●	●	●	● CON		Edrington Group
GLENMORANGIE	●	●	●	●	●	●	●	●	●	●	●	●	●		Glenmorangie Plc
GRANTS	●	●	●	●	●	●	●	●	●	●	●	●	●		William Grant & Sons
JAMESON	●	●	●	●	●	●	●	●	●	●	●	●	●		Perno Ricard
TEACHERS	○	●	●	●	●	●	●	●	●	●	●	●	● CON		Allied Domecq
WHYTE & MACKAY	●	●	●	●	●	●	●	●	●	●	●	●	●		Fortune Brands

Column labels (diagonal): ENVIRONMENTAL REPORTING, POLLUTION, NUCLEAR POWER, OTHER, ANIMAL TESTING, FACTORY FARMING, OTHER ANIMAL RIGHTS, OPPRESSIVE REGIMES, WORKERS' RIGHTS, IRRESPONSIBLE MARKETING, ARMAMENTS, GENETIC ENGINEERING, BOYCOTT CALL, POLITICAL DONATIONS

Key

- ● Top rating (no criticisms found)
- ○ Middle rating
- ● Bottom rating
- ◐ A related company has a bottom rating and the company itself has a middle rating
- ◯ A related company has a middle rating
- ● A related company has a bottom rating

Source: ECRA-See page 14 for full key to symbols.

GOOD SHOPPING GUIDE 2003 ETHICAL
- Glenmorangie
- Grants

- Famous Grouse
- Jameson
- Whyte & Mackay

- Bells
- Teachers

Breathe in London

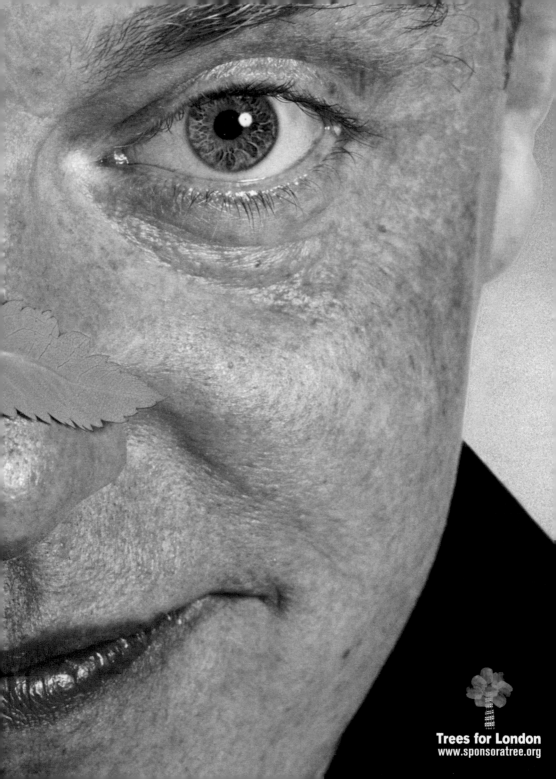

Trees for London
www.sponsoratree.org

Yoghurt

With the ever-growing popularity of yoghurt it is good to keep asking questions about ingredients and the welfare of the animals producing the milk.

THE CASE FOR ORGANIC

Organic-standard yoghurt is not only better for the consumer but better for the milk-producing cow. According to the Soil Association, calves on organic farms will have been suckled for around nine weeks, rather than separated from their mothers within a few days, and the disease rates of animals are lower because of better husbandry and a diet of mostly grass and clover. Organic cows are not kept permanently shut up indoors throughout the winter as non-organic herds often are. Goat and sheep yoghurt also comes from less intensive conditions as it is produced by smaller companies; it is also important for the ten per cent of the population who are lactose-intolerant.

LIVE YOGHURT

Live yoghurts contain two species of bacteria naturally found in the human gut which can, unlike ordinary yoghurt bacteria, pass via the stomach into the intestines, with the claimed benefits of improving digestion and helping to prevent colon cancer. In fact, for people who are already fit, the benefits are probably marginal, but live yoghurt is almost certainly very beneficial for people who are recovering from a stomach bug or who are taking antibiotics.

GELATINE

Gelatine may be added to thicken fat-reduced yoghurts and so vegetarians should keep a careful eye on the ingredients list.

NON-DAIRY

Most non-dairy yoghurts are made from soya and as such will be highly processed and may contain salt, sugar and other additives, but they contain the same bacterial cultures as conventional yoghurt. As some soya is from GM sources, you may be best advised to look for organic products or those labelled as non-GM.

ALTERNATIVES

You can make your own yoghurt by buying a pot of live yoghurt, adding milk and leaving it in a warm place. It works equally well for soya yoghurts. The system can go on almost indefinitely, but consult a reliable recipe book for useful tips about storage and hygiene.

- Rachel's Dairy
- Yeo Valley Organic

- Muller
- Onken
- Provamel Yofu
- Total
- Woodlands Park

- Danone
- Ski
- St Ivel Shape
- Weight Watchers

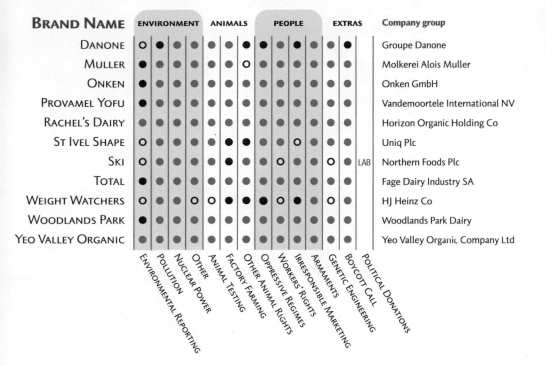

Brand Name	Environment: Environmental Reporting	Environment: Pollution	Environment: Nuclear Power	Environment: Other	Animals: Animal Testing	Animals: Factory Farming	Animals: Other Animal Rights	People: Oppressive Regimes	People: Workers' Rights	People: Irresponsible Marketing	People: Armaments	Extras: Genetic Engineering	Extras: Boycott Call	Extras: Political Donations	Company group
Danone	○	●	•	•	•	•	●	●	•	●	•	•	●		Groupe Danone
Muller	●	•	•	•	•	•	○	•	•	•	•	•	•		Molkerei Alois Muller
Onken	●	•	•	•	•	•	•	•	•	•	•	•	•		Onken GmbH
Provamel Yofu	●	•	•	•	•	•	•	•	•	•	•	•	•		Vandemoortele International NV
Rachel's Dairy	•	•	•	•	•	•	•	•	•	•	•	•	•		Horizon Organic Holding Co
St Ivel Shape	○	•	•	•	•	●	●	•	•	○	•	•	•		Uniq Plc
Ski	○	•	•	•	•	●	•	•	○	•	•	○	•	LAB	Northern Foods Plc
Total	●	•	•	•	•	•	•	•	•	•	•	•	•		Fage Dairy Industry SA
Weight Watchers	○	•	•	○	○	●	●	●	○	●	•	○	•		HJ Heinz Co
Woodlands Park	●	•	•	•	•	•	•	•	•	•	•	•	•		Woodlands Park Dairy
Yeo Valley Organic	•	•	•	•	•	•	•	•	•	•	•	•	•		Yeo Valley Organic Company Ltd

Key
- • Top rating (no criticisms found)
- ○ Middle rating
- ● Bottom rating
- A related company has a bottom rating and the company itself has a middle rating
- A related company has a middle rating
- A related company has a bottom rating

Source: ECRA-See page 14 for full key to symbols.

Sugar

Most of us know that too much sugar is bad for us, but we would find it hard to live without it. The main thing to remember is that too much processing removes its most nutritious elements. Other factors to consider are the livelihoods of workers in fields and factories who have helped bring the sugar to our supermarkets, where our sugar comes from and who has been benefiting from the recent changes in the world trade rules.

HEALTH FACTORS

Processed white sugar supplies our bodies with little more than cheap calories. If we take too much we risk not only tooth decay but other long-term problems such as diabetes, dyspepsia and heart and liver disease. Too much sugar can even affect our concentration.

Some scientists argue that we are abusing the evolutionary role of our sweet tooth by consuming refined sugar. Our ancestors would have satisfied their cravings for sweetness by eating fruit and sweet vegetables, and in so doing would have obtained necessary nutrients like vitamin C. In places where sugar cane is eaten raw, people have healthy teeth because of the vitamins and minerals that occur naturally in the juice.

Unrefined or raw brown sugars have been processed to some degree but they retain more nutrients than white sugar. Any superior brown sugar will have been derived from cane. Brown sugar from beet has been coloured with caramel or molasses.

FREE TRADE

Although we would normally argue in favour of locally-grown produce over imports, a special case can be made for sugar cane because of its importance to the poorer economies of the world. The movement towards free trade mapped out by the World Trade Organisation aims to eliminate the guaranteed quotas and prices for sugar producers in countries like Jamaica, the Philippines and Mauritius. A report published in 1999 stated that the economic situation for small and medium-sized sugar planters in the Philippines had seriously deteriorated over the last few years.

The Sugar Register of FLO (Fairtrade Labelling Organisations International) – which is used for the UK's Fair Trade Mark – has encountered difficulties in setting certification standards. Accepted criteria normally operate on the basis of the need of disadvantaged Third World farmers, which rules out poor-country sugar producers as they already get preferential treatment (higher prices) from the EU.

Most of the socially-conscious companies buy their sugar from Mauritius, which has a relatively progressive and equitable system in place. Its Sugar Syndicate pays the same pro rata rate whether the sugar comes from a large estate or from one of 30,000 smallholdings. As things stand at the moment, the existence of the Syndicate rules out schemes to benefit individual disadvantaged growers, which is another requirement for Fairtrade Mark certification, but the Sugar Register has been looking for a way round this problem.

ORGANIC

The traditional practice of cold pressing sugar cane is being used by a German company called Rapunzel. It pays a premium to Brazilian farmers to produce an organic product it calls Rapadura, which has a mild caramel-like flavour and retains all the nutrients of the sugar cane. It is suitable for baking and has a powdery consistency. Sucanat and Syramena are two other brands, available through some wholefood stores, that have undergone minimal processing.

- Traidcraft
- Whitworths

- Billingtons

- Silver Spoon
- Tate & Lyle

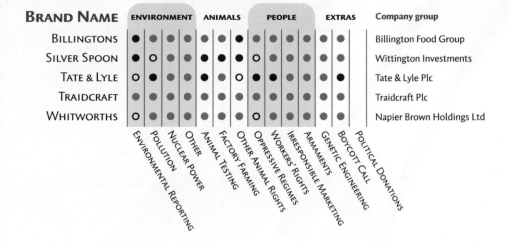

BRAND NAME	ENVIRONMENT				ANIMALS			PEOPLE				EXTRAS			Company group
	Environmental Reporting	Pollution	Nuclear Power	Other	Animal Testing	Factory Farming	Other Animal Rights	Oppressive Regimes	Workers' Rights	Irresponsible Marketing	Armaments	Genetic Engineering	Boycott Call	Political Donations	
BILLINGTONS	●	●	●	●	●	●	●	●	●	●	●	●	●		Billington Food Group
SILVER SPOON	●	○	●	●	●	●		○	●	●	●	●	●		Wittington Investments
TATE & LYLE	○	●	●	●	●	●	○	●	●	●	●	●	●		Tate & Lyle Plc
TRAIDCRAFT	●	●	●	●	●	●		●	●	●	●	●	●		Traidcraft Plc
WHITWORTHS	○	●	●	●	●	●		○	●	●	●	●	●		Napier Brown Holdings Ltd

Key

● Top rating (no criticisms found)

○ Middle rating

● Bottom rating

● A related company has a bottom rating and the company itself has a middle rating

○ A related company has a middle rating

● A related company has a bottom rating

Source: ECRA-See page 14 for full key to symbols.

153

Soup

Packet soups and canned soups may seem like a good and quick form of nutrition, but we should think again before buying. Their nutritional value varies and some of the companies making them have poor ethical records.

HEALTHY DIETS

Like many types of processed foods, ready-made soups have been criticised for often containing high levels of sugars, salt and artificial additives such as flavourings and thickeners. Packet soups have been most heavily condemned for containing little of nutritional value, while canned soups often use high levels of sugar and thickeners. Fresh carton soups are often a healthier option but many still have a high salt content.

Home-made soups made with organic vegetables and with sparing use of salt make healthy, filling and balanced meals. If made in large quantities, they can be easily refrigerated or frozen.

COMPANIES

Consolidation in the food industry means that supermarket shoppers are faced with an array of companies with problematic ethical records, while the smaller companies and brands are being squeezed out of the mass markets.

Apart from the vegetarian companies Suma and Just Wholefoods, all of the companies included here have connections with factory farming.

Although the issue of the irresponsible marketing of baby foods and breastmilk substitutes usually focuses on the activities of Nestlé, Heinz has also been the subject of sustained and serious criticisms on the subject from campaigning organisations such as Baby Milk Action. It has been criticised for violations of the International Code of Marketing of Breastmilk Substitutes in countries including Pakistan, Uganda, Peru, Mexico, Ghana and Malaysia. Farleys, a Heinz subsidiary, was also cited back in 1994 as having produced marketing material which played on the insecurities of women by claiming that breastfeeding harmed the sex lives of many new mothers, and that 'modern women' regarded breasts as 'more than just feeding machines'. Fortunately, we have not found the same claims in recent Farley's marketing materials.

ORGANIC ISSUES

Suma and Just Wholefoods both sell only organic brands of soup, and the New Covent Garden Soup Company has brought out a range of organic choices. Other than these, all the products concerned are made from non-organic produce, which generally involves the use of pesticides and potentially environmentally-damaging growing systems.

Packaging is another issue, as ready-made soup comes either in packets, tins or cartons. None of the products examined had any indication that they were packaged in recycled materials.

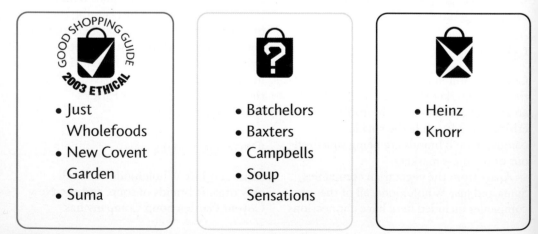

GOOD SHOPPING GUIDE 2003 ETHICAL

- Just Wholefoods
- New Covent Garden
- Suma

- Batchelors
- Baxters
- Campbells
- Soup Sensations

- Heinz
- Knorr

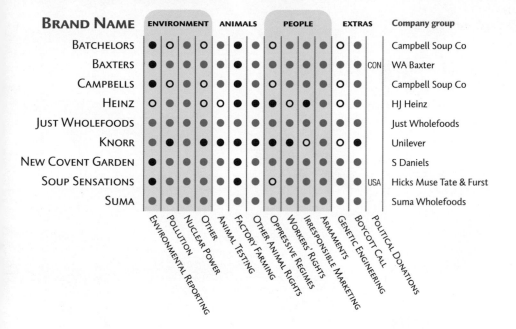

BRAND NAME	ENVIRONMENT				ANIMALS			PEOPLE				EXTRAS			Company group
	Environmental Reporting	Pollution	Nuclear Power	Other	Animal Testing	Factory Farming	Other Animal Rights	Oppressive Regimes	Workers' Rights	Irresponsible Marketing	Armaments	Genetic Engineering	Boycott Call	Political Donations	
BATCHELORS															Campbell Soup Co
BAXTERS													CON		WA Baxter
CAMPBELLS															Campbell Soup Co
HEINZ															HJ Heinz
JUST WHOLEFOODS															Just Wholefoods
KNORR															Unilever
NEW COVENT GARDEN															S Daniels
SOUP SENSATIONS													USA		Hicks Muse Tate & Furst
SUMA															Suma Wholefoods

Key

● Top rating (no criticisms found)

○ Middle rating

● Bottom rating

◐ A related company has a bottom rating and the
company itself has a middle rating

○ A related company has a middle rating

● A related company has a bottom rating

Source: ECRA–See page 14 for full key to symbols.

Baby food

Everyone wants the 'best for baby', and that usually means the most natural available forms of care and nutrition. Luckily there has long been a high level of awareness and responsibility about the marketing of baby milk substitutes and of baby foods in general. Companies are of course eager to promote their products as the best in the market, but as always it helps to study the details. Parents not only have to consider carefully when to introduce baby to different foods but also need to have confidence in the brands they choose from the shelves.

BREAST MILK SUBSTITUTES

The WHO/UNICEF International Code of Marketing of Breast Milk Substitutes has been developed in response to serious criticisms of the marketing practices of baby milk/food manufacturers over many years. Because of the massive amount of evidence in favour of prolonged breastfeeding, the Code lays down various guidelines, including that solid foods be labelled as only suitable from six months. In poorer countries in particular, moving from breastmilk to substitutes can have the severest consequences for babies' health. In the late 1990s there were serious breaches of the Code. (Contact Baby Milk Action for more information on this subject: 01223 464420)

DIFFERENT KINDS OF FOODS

Baby food comes in three main types:

- 'wet' foods, which are pre-cooked and puréed meals packaged in jars or cans
- 'dry' foods, in boxes or sachets, which have to be rehydrated to make meals
- cereals, rusks and rice cakes, eaten plain or with milk.

The companies reviewed here produce all three types, except for Farleys, Milupa and Olvarit, which, at the time of research, only produce dry varieties.

ORGANIC BRANDS

Parents are increasingly looking for organic food for their babies. There are now exclusively organic companies like Baby Organix and Hipp, while Heinz and Boots also do their own organic ranges. *The Organic Baby Book* (*www.theorganicbabybook.co.uk*) lists the different brands available in the UK. One strong argument in favour of using organic food for babies is that they are more vulnerable than adults to toxins such as pesticide residues.

LABELLING & PACKAGING

Since 1999 there has been legislation in Britain setting compulsory standards for the nutritional value and labelling of baby foods. The regulations set minimum quantities for the main vitamins, minerals and protein, and maximum quantities for fats, carbohydrate and sodium. All the baby food examined for this report did comply with these regulations.

An EC survey found that most of the packaging for baby foods is in theory recyclable but that very little attention is drawn to this fact.

ALTERNATIVES & NICHE BRANDS

Baby food can of course be made at home. One good and healthy process is to liquidise or sieve cooked fruit or vegetables, preferably organic ones of course. Some good baby food recipe books

are available, including *Cooking for Your Baby* (Laraine Toms, Penguin), *Complete New Guide to Preparing Babyfoods* (Sue Castle, Bantam) and *The New Vegetarian Baby* (Baird and Yntema, McBooks).

Yoghurt and fromage frais makers have entered the baby food market, with varieties labelled as being suitable from four to six months. There are also niche brands such as Mother Nature Babyfoods (which produces halal foods), Original Fresh Babyfood Co and Osska (both of these make fresh meals which are sold in the cold cabinets of health food stores and supermarkets).

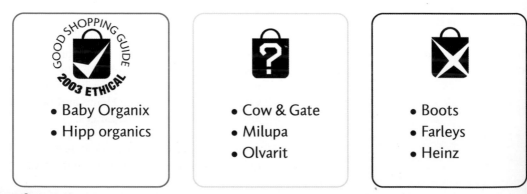

- Baby Organix
- Hipp organics

- Cow & Gate
- Milupa
- Olvarit

- Boots
- Farleys
- Heinz

BRAND NAME	ENVIRONMENT	ANIMALS	PEOPLE	EXTRAS	Company group

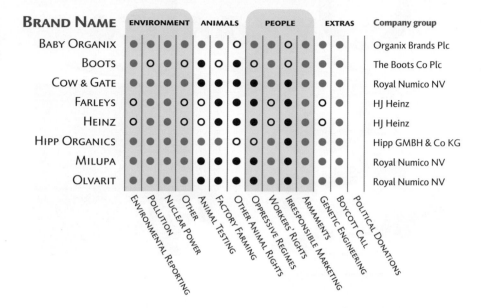

BRAND NAME	Company group
BABY ORGANIX	Organix Brands Plc
BOOTS	The Boots Co Plc
COW & GATE	Royal Numico NV
FARLEYS	HJ Heinz
HEINZ	HJ Heinz
HIPP ORGANICS	Hipp GMBH & Co KG
MILUPA	Royal Numico NV
OLVARIT	Royal Numico NV

Column headings (angled):
ENVIRONMENTAL REPORTING · POLLUTION · NUCLEAR POWER · OTHER · ANIMAL TESTING · FACTORY FARMING · OTHER ANIMAL RIGHTS · OPPRESSIVE REGIMES · WORKERS' RIGHTS · IRRESPONSIBLE MARKETING · ARMAMENTS · GENETIC ENGINEERING · BOYCOTT CALL · POLITICAL DONATIONS

Key

● Top rating (no criticisms found)

○ Middle rating

● Bottom rating

◉ A related company has a bottom rating and the company itself has a middle rating

○ A related company has a middle rating

● A related company has a bottom rating

Source: ECRA-See page 14 for full key to symbols.

Organico

delivering the best in organics

organico, Tel: 0118 9510 518 - www.organico.co.uk

Pasta

Tagliatelli, linguine, fusilli, or just good old spaghetti, whichever kind you fancy, the artistic shapes of pasta are always popular whether in salads or as the basis of delicious and varied main dishes – with tomato, seafood or meat sauces. Although most of the different kinds of pasta available are equally healthy, we can always go one better and look for organic and/or fresh varieties. With some practice, you can even try to make your own.

PURE WHEAT

Traditional quality pasta should be made with 100 per cent durum wheat, in wholewheat or semolina form. However, with the growth in the own-brand market pushing prices down, many of the cheaper pastas now contain 'soft wheat' substitutes, which can result in a slightly sticky or slimy texture.

A richer pasta is produced with the addition of egg, which vegans inevitably avoid. Tomato or spinach is added to produce the distinctive red or green pastas, and some pasta-makers are fond of ingredients like nettles, beetroot and chilli.

FRESH PASTA

In Italy, fresh pasta is available in over a hundred variations of shape and filling, and it is sold in specialist shops to be eaten on the day of purchase. In the UK, most of the fresh pasta available is not quite that fresh, as preservation in a modified environment is usual to extend the shelf life. Some from specialist shops is very good, but at the same time many of the fully-prepared fresh pasta meals on the supermarket shelves are rather over-stodgy with not many authentic ingredients.

Fresh pasta most often contains egg, which again is not good news for vegans, and if the pasta is from a non-organic company the eggs will probably be from battery farms. All brands certified as organic by the Soil Association will contain only free-range eggs.

ORGANIC, WHOLE WHEAT AND GM

As the supermarket own-brands are responsible for more than three quarters of all UK pasta sales, the introduction of organic own-brand pasta ranges is a positive step towards sustainable agriculture.

We need to be wary of wholewheat pasta varieties (unless they are clearly marked as organic) because they are far more likely to contain chemical residues, as the husk or bran of the wheat absorbs more of the pesticides and fertilisers than the semolina used alone in white varieties.

As there are no GM varieties cleared for sale within the EU, dry pasta in its standard form should be GM-free, with the possible exception of the red, tomato pasta which could contain GM tomato paste. All the pasta certified as organic by the Soil Association is sure to be GM-free.

PACKAGING

Most pasta is packaged in polypropylene, which although recyclable will usually end up in landfill. Given the expansion of the dried product during cooking and the need for thicker packaging for fresh pasta (in order to maintain the seal around the modified environment), far greater volumes of plastic are needed for the fresh product.

ALTERNATIVES

For those with wheat or gluten intolerances, Orgran produces a rice pasta which has been produced in isolation from all other foodstuffs. Another possible alternative may be one of the speciality pastas produced by Terra e Cielo, which are made from farro wheat or 'spelt' (an ancient forerunner to modern wheat), which contains considerably less gluten and which the company claims may be suitable for people with a mild wheat intolerance.

An alternative to expensive fresh pasta is to make your own, starting with lasagne, which can be made by rolling out flour and water in the right quantities.

- Barilla
- Dellugo
- Fiorucci
- La Terra e Cielo
- Orgran
- Pastificio Rana
- Puglisi

- Meridian
- Morrisons
- Safeway

- Asda
- Buitoni
- Marks & Spencer
- Marshalls
- Sainsbury
- Seeds of Change
- Sitoni
- Tesco

Brand Name	Environment				Animals			People				Extras			Company group
Asda													USA		Walmart Stores Inc
Barilla															Guido M Brarilla
Buitoni															Nestle
Dellugo															UGO Foods Group
Fiorucci															Cesare Fiorucci SpA
La Terra e Cielo															Co-op Terra e Cielo
Marks & Spencer													CON		Marks & Spencer
Marshalls															Doughty Hanson
Meridian															Greencore
Morrisons															Wm Morrisons
Orgran															Roma Food Products
Pastificio Rana															Pastificio Rana SpA
Puglisi															Puglisi (UK) Ltd
Safeway															Safeway Plc
Sainsbury													LAB		J Sainsbury Plc
Seeds of Change															Mars Inc
Sitoni															Doughty Hanson
Tesco															Tesco Plc

Column categories (left to right): ENVIRONMENTAL REPORTING, POLLUTION, NUCLEAR POWER, OTHER (Environment); ANIMAL TESTING, FACTORY FARMING, OTHER ANIMAL RIGHTS (Animals); OPPRESSIVE REGIMES, WORKERS' RIGHTS, IRRESPONSIBLE MARKETING, ARMAMENTS (People); GENETIC ENGINEERING, BOYCOTT CALL, POLITICAL DONATIONS (Extras)

Key

● Top rating (no criticisms found)

○ Middle rating

● Bottom rating

◕ A related company has a bottom rating and the company itself has a middle rating

○ A related company has a middle rating

● A related company has a bottom rating

Source: ECRA-See page 14 for full key to symbols.

Cooking oil

With olive oil being touted as an antidote to ageing, there's little wonder that nearly every granny now pours it over her salads. But we should be aware that the great rush to expand production in Mediterranean countries is threatening the local ecology and causing serious soil erosion. So it's best to buy organic if you can, it's even more delicious and better for the environment. Here, we look at the major branded cooking oils, including supermarket own-brands.

TROUBLE IN SPAIN

An important advantage of most olive oil is that it is almost certain to be GM-free, but the food and development organisation Sustain reports that over-intensification of olive oil production in Spain has resulted in erosion and other agronomic and environmental problems, causing irreversible damage in over 40 per cent of Andalucia. The new methods of production have also involved increasing the use of herbicides, pesticides and fungicides. Sustain recommends that consumers choose organic olive oil wherever possible.

PURITY AT A COST

Most of the UK's oilseed rape is grown as a winter crop, which Sustain argues has had a detrimental effect on Britain's environment, causing biodiversity to suffer and bird populations to decline. Winter crops have also at times provided an excuse for mass shooting of wood pigeons.

Although British farmers are not likely to be introducing GM crops yet, the whole GM issue remains important with cooking oils, simply because much of our oil is imported and because most of the major oil seeds have already been the targets of experimentation. Worryingly for consumers concerned with GM issues, vegetable oil produced from GM plants does not have to be labelled as GM – this is because the processing of oils means that neither protein nor DNA is thought to be present. Those who want to avoid any GM link should opt for sunflower oil, olive oil or organic oils. We should be aware that maize oil, soya oil and canola (rapeseed) oils may be processed from GM plants, especially if they originate from Canada. Some companies are trying to source their vegetable oils from GM-free crops, but progress has been patchy.
Consumers can ask their stores for their policy on GM oil.

OWN-BRAND OILS

Most supermarkets refuse to say which companies produce their own-brand cooking oils. Pressure from consumers may change this policy eventually, but until we can be certain of the identity of the own-brand suppliers, the brands will continue to be rated with the supermarket. Unlike other companies, supermarkets are rated according to their stocking policies.

PACKAGING

More expensive oils are likely to be in glass bottles, which are easy to recycle. But products in the lower price range are almost always packaged in plastic bottles, some of which may be made from PVC (which is identifiable by a '3' inside a recycling symbol on the base of the bottle). Plastic recycling in the UK is still very poorly developed, with about 95 per cent of it still being landfilled or incinerated.

60-SECOND GREEN GUIDE

- Buy glass bottles in preference to plastic ones
- There is little risk of active GM materials being present in any oil
- For the least risk of GM 'contamination', use olive oil
- Most vegetable oils are equally good for you

- Filippo Berio
- Pura
- Suma

- Marks & Spencer
- Meridian
- Princes
- Safeway
- Sainsbury

- Asda
- Crisp & Dry
- Flora
- Mazola
- Olivio
- Tesco

Brand Name	Environment	Animals	People	Extras		Company group
Asda					USA	Wal-Mart Stores Plc
Crisp & Dry						Unilever
Filippo Berio						RH Amar
Flora						Unilever
Marks & Spencer					CON	Marks & Spencer Plc
Mazola						Unilever
Meridian						Greencore Group
Olivio						Unilever
Princes						Mitsubishi
Pura						Pura Plc
Safeway						Safeway Plc
Sainsbury					LAB	J Sainsbury Plc
Suma						Suma Wholefoods
Tesco						Tesco Plc

Column labels: Environmental Reporting, Pollution, Nuclear Power, Other, Animal Testing, Factory Farming, Other Animal Rights, Oppressive Regimes, Workers' Rights, Irresponsible Marketing, Armaments, Genetic Engineering, Boycott Call, Political Donations

Key

- ● Top rating (no criticisms found)
- ○ Middle rating
- ● Bottom rating
- ◉ A related company has a bottom rating and the company itself has a middle rating
- ○ A related company has a middle rating
- ● A related company has a bottom rating

Source: ECRA-See page 14 for full key to symbols.

ORGANIC BUTTER

Organic cows get better treatment than most – because they are never kept permanently indoors, which keeps them healthier, and their calves are suckled for around nine weeks.

GM ISSUES

Many spreads and spreadable butters contain soya oils, which may be labelled simply as vegetable oil or fat. Many of these may be from GM soya beans. That's why it's better to look for products labelled as GM-free or organic.

Lecithin is a common additive derived from soya, and if it is of GM origin it need not be labelled as such on the grounds that there will be no DNA present.

Butter may not be unaffected by the GM issue, as the cows may have been given GM feed. Only organically-certified products will avoid GM entirely.

PACKAGING

Butter normally comes wrapped in a single piece of paper, and this is clearly better than the plastic tub packaging used for margarine and spreads. Although the tubs are marked as recyclable, how many of us actually do recycle them? If you are concerned you should contact your local authority to ask about recycling facilities.

BUTTER
- Anchor
- Castle Dairies
- Yeo Valley

MARGARINE
- GranoVita
- Pure
- Suma

BUTTER
- Kerrygold
- St Ivel Shirgar

MARGARINE
- Clover
- Utterly Butterly
- Vitalite

BUTTER
- Harmonie
- Lurpak

MARGARINE
- Benecol
- Flora
- Granose
- I Can't Believe it's Not Butter

Brand Name	ENVIRONMENT				ANIMALS			PEOPLE				EXTRAS			Company group
	Environmental Reporting	Pollution	Nuclear Power	Other	Animal Testing	Factory Farming	Other Animal Rights	Oppressive Regimes	Workers' Rights	Irresponsible Marketing	Armaments	Genetic Engineering	Boycott Call	Political Donations	
BUTTER															
Anchor	●	●	●	●	●	●	●	●	●	●	●	●	●	●	Rank Group Ltd (New Zealand)
Castle Dairies	●	●	●	●	●	○		●	●	●	●	●	●	●	Castle Dairies Ltd
Harmonie	●	○	●	●	●	○	●	●	○	●	●	●	●	●	Arla Foods AMBA
Kerrygold	●	●	●	●	●	●	●	●	●	●	●	●	●	●	Irish Dairy Board Cooperative Ltd
Lurpak	●	○	●	●	●	○	●	●	○	●	●	●	●	●	Arla Foods AMBA
St Ivel Shirgar	●	●	●	●	●	●	●	●	●	●	●	●	●	●	Dairy Crest Group Plc
Yeo Valley	●	●	●	●	●	●	●	●	●	●	●	●	●	●	Yeo Valley Organic Company Ltd
MARGARINES & SPREADS															
Benecol	●	●	●	●	●	●	●	●	●	●	●	●	●	● (USA)	Johnson & Johnson
Clover	●	●	●	●	●	●	●	●	●	●	●	●	●	●	Dairy Crest Group Plc
Flora	●	●	●	●	●	●	●	●	●	○	●	○	●	●	Unilever
Granose	●	●	●	●	●	●	●	○	●	●	●	●	●	● (USA)	Archer Daniels Midland Co
GranoVita	○	●	●	●	●	●	●	●	●	●	●	●	●	●	De-Vau-Ge Gesundkostwerk
I Can't Believe INB	●	●	●	●	●	●	●	●	●	○	●	○	●	●	Unilever
Pure	●	●	●	●	●	●	●	●	●	●	●	●	●	●	Matthews Group Ltd
Suma	●	●	●	●	●	●	●	●	●	●	●	●	●	●	Suma Wholefoods
Utterly Butterly	○	●	●	●	●	●	●	●	●	○	●	●	●	●	Uniq Plc
Vitalite	○	●	●	●	●	●	●	●	●	○	●	●	●	●	Uniq Plc

Key

● Top rating (no criticisms found)

○ Middle rating

● Bottom rating

◐ A related company has a bottom rating and the company itself has a middle rating

○ A related company has a middle rating

● A related company has a bottom rating

Source: ECRA-See page 14 for full key to symbols.

Breakfast cereals

There was a time, not long ago, when breakfast food manufacturers seemed to rule our lives. First thing in the morning, mums, dads and kids alike were easily persuaded that those first mouthfuls of cornflakes, sugar and milk were like manna from heaven. But the age of innocence is well and truly over.

A HEALTHY START?

Breakfast cereals have long been a neat way for the food companies to take perfectly healthy food apart and put it back together again for profit. Inevitably these foods lose much of their nutritional benefit in the process, which is why the companies have to add all those vitamins again at the end, claiming that these make their product healthier and more special than any others.

Some companies make healthy eating claims about their products which are not, according to the Food Commission, substantiated with proper evidence. There was concern when Kellogg's claimed that they were 'serving the nation's health' while their Corn Flakes had been found to contain one of the highest salt levels on the cereals market. In 1998 the National Food Alliance found that some breakfast cereals were ten per cent saltier than sea water. (See relevent ECRA Research Supplement for details).

SWEETENING THE KIDDIES

The children's cereals sector makes up about a third of the British market for breakfast cereals, and that is why many products like Quaker's Sugar Puffs are deliberately packaged to attract children. Such products can be high in salt as well as low in fibre. One food author has complained that with sugar accounting for up to half the weight of the ingredients some products are 'twice as sweet as a jam doughnut'.

OTHER CONCERNS

Pesticide residues are regularly detected in corn-based cereals even after processing, and research has shown that these residues find their way into 10-30 per cent of conventional breakfast cereals.

Until the tide turned against GM products, there was considerable doubt about the GM content of products made from soya or maize. Now Kellogg's products are reportedly free from proteins from GM crops. Weetabix Ltd stated that no GM ingredient, additive or derivatives are used in any of its processes. Quaker

Oats Ltd claimed that it does not use ingredients containing GM material in any Quaker product and that it had tested all lecithin used in its products to ensure freedom from any such material; the company also said it would only consider using ingredients derived from GM crops in the longer term if they had been fully approved by the relevant regulatory and scientific authorities.

- Doves Farm
- Infinity
- Jordans
- Mornflake
- Whole Earth

- Kallo
- Kashi
- Kellogg's
- Weetabix

- Quaker Oats
- Shredded Wheat

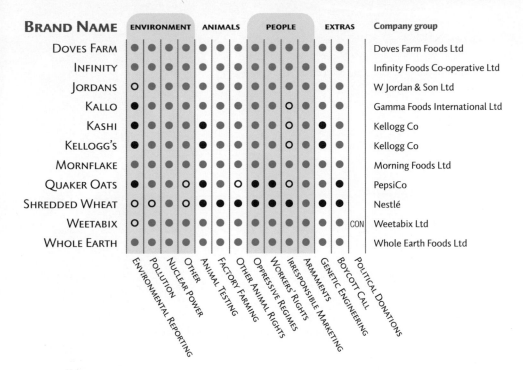

BRAND NAME	ENVIRONMENT	ANIMALS	PEOPLE	EXTRAS	Company group
DOVES FARM					Doves Farm Foods Ltd
INFINITY					Infinity Foods Co-operative Ltd
JORDANS					W Jordan & Son Ltd
KALLO					Gamma Foods International Ltd
KASHI					Kellogg Co
KELLOGG'S					Kellogg Co
MORNFLAKE					Morning Foods Ltd
QUAKER OATS					PepsiCo
SHREDDED WHEAT					Nestlé
WEETABIX			CON		Weetabix Ltd
WHOLE EARTH					Whole Earth Foods Ltd

Column headings (left to right): ENVIRONMENTAL REPORTING, POLLUTION, NUCLEAR POWER, OTHER, ANIMAL TESTING, FACTORY FARMING, OTHER ANIMAL RIGHTS, OPPRESSIVE REGIMES, WORKERS' RIGHTS, IRRESPONSIBLE MARKETING, ARMAMENTS, GENETIC ENGINEERING, BOYCOTT CALL, POLITICAL DONATIONS

Key

- ● Top rating (no criticisms found)
- ○ Middle rating
- ● Bottom rating
- ◉ A related company has a bottom rating and the company itself has a middle rating
- ⦾ A related company has a middle rating
- ● A related company has a bottom rating

Source: ECRA-See page 14 for full key to symbols.

Jams & spreads

Although home-made jams, marmalade, lemon curd and other spreads usually have much better ingredients than those on the supermarket shelves, few of us have the time or opportunity to make the stuff. So if you want to have the healthiest spreads for breakfast and tea-time you need first to have a look at what goes into the shop varieties. The volume leaders are Robertsons and Chivers-Hartley, while Chivers-Hartley is also the largest own-brand maker. Baxters and Duerrs make own-brands too.

FRUIT LEVELS

To be called jam, a preserve needs only to have a minimum of 35 per cent fruit content, while marmalade can have as little as 20 per cent fruit. We should be aware that in many commercial jams some of the fruit can be from frozen or concentrate sources. Also the fruit and sugar is heavily boiled, which reduces the nutritional value.

Extra jam has 45g of fruit per 100g. Compôtes are preserves with very high fruit levels, so they do not set in the same way as traditional jam, but they retain much more of the nutritional value of the fruit.

OTHER INGREDIENTS

To be called jam or marmalade, a preserve has to have at least 60g of sugar per 100g of product – even for the extra-fruit varieties. Reduced-sugar jams have 30-55g, but will often have added colour, emulsifier, preservative and stabiliser. Fruit spreads are usually purely derived from fruit, relying on

a fruit juice such as apple for sweetness. This means they are best kept in the fridge as they do not keep as long as sugar-rich jam or marmalade.

Artificial sweeteners may be used in 'diet' products, under a variety of guises such as aspartame, saccharin or xylitol. In higher fruit-content products, preservatives may be used. Preservatives such as potassium sorbate (E200-213) are suspected of causing allergic reactions, gastric irritations and problems with conception in some people. Manufacturers could avoid using them by noting a shorter shelf life and recommending refrigeration.

Lemon curd contains eggs, which are likely to be battery-produced except in the case of organic products. Some jellies and jams may contain gelatine, an animal by-product, to aid with setting.

No genetically engineered fruit is permitted in the UK but the enzymes used to process the fruit, gelatine or added sweeteners could have involved GM. Choosing organic products allows us to avoid all these additives. The only brand that is exclusively organic is Bionova. Other companies, such as Meridian, Whole Earth, Hartleys (Wm P Hartley brand) and Baxters, make some organic jams. The Herb Stall was the only organic lemon curd producer found at the time of the survey.

PACKAGING

Although most fruit preserves are packed in glass jars, there has been some use of squeezy plastic bottles or pouches by companies like Hartleys and Robertsons. Some honey manufacturers are starting to pack their products in rigid plastic jars, and this could happen in the jam market too.

- Bionova
- The Herb Stall
- Whole Earth

- Baxters
- Bonne Maman
- Duerr's
- Stute
- Tiptree

- Chivers
- Frank Cooper
- Hartley's
- Meridian
- Robertsons

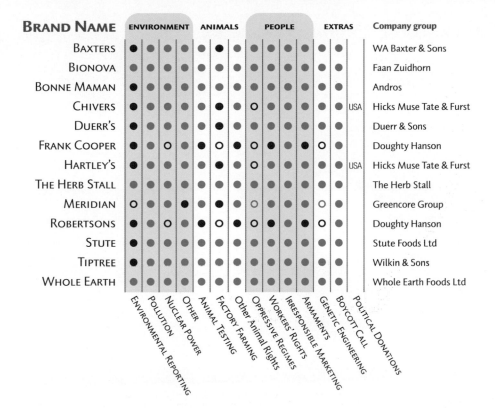

BRAND NAME	Company group
BAXTERS	WA Baxter & Sons
BIONOVA	Faan Zuidhorn
BONNE MAMAN	Andros
CHIVERS	Hicks Muse Tate & Furst
DUERR'S	Duerr & Sons
FRANK COOPER	Doughty Hanson
HARTLEY'S	Hicks Muse Tate & Furst
THE HERB STALL	The Herb Stall
MERIDIAN	Greencore Group
ROBERTSONS	Doughty Hanson
STUTE	Stute Foods Ltd
TIPTREE	Wilkin & Sons
WHOLE EARTH	Whole Earth Foods Ltd

Column groups: ENVIRONMENT, ANIMALS, PEOPLE, EXTRAS

Columns: ENVIRONMENTAL REPORTING, POLLUTION, NUCLEAR POWER, OTHER, ANIMAL TESTING, FACTORY FARMING, OTHER ANIMAL RIGHTS, OPPRESSIVE REGIMES, WORKERS' RIGHTS, IRRESPONSIBLE MARKETING, ARMAMENTS, GENETIC ENGINEERING, BOYCOTT CALL, POLITICAL DONATIONS

Key

- ● Top rating (no criticisms found)
- ○ Middle rating
- ● Bottom rating
- ◐ A related company has a bottom rating and the company itself has a middle rating
- ◯ A related company has a middle rating
- ● A related company has a bottom rating

Source: ECRA–See page 14 for full key to symbols.

Bread

Home baking is one sure way to guarantee your bread is free from additives and plastic packaging. In the shops, wholemeal organic is the answer.

CHEMICALS AND ADDITIVES

Sliced and wrapped loaves are by far the biggest-selling kind of bread, representing 80 per cent of bread consumption. The main manufacturers are Allied Bakeries and British Bakeries, each controlling about a third of the market. Allied make Kingsmill and British Bakeries make Hovis. The biggest bakery specialist is Greggs, which controls the Bakers Oven, Olivers, Bartletts and Crawfords outlets, as well as Greggs stores.

Since 1961, plant bakeries have used a fast-track production system known as the Chorleywood Bread Process (CBP). It replaces the traditional slow fermentation with a short burst in high-speed mixers, using much greater quantities of yeast. More water is absorbed into the dough, which rises up and reaches its desired volume more quickly. There are many additives, including chemical 'improvers' which oxidise newly-milled flour. Because the bleaches used to whiten and sterilise the flour manage to strip much of the nutritional value, vitamins and minerals have to be added back in.

The drawback of conventional wholemeal bread, in which the whole of the wheatgrain is retained, is that higher levels of residues of fertilisers, pesticides and post-harvest storage treatment chemicals are present in wholemeal than in ordinary white or brown flour. This is a very good reason to choose organic bread.

ALTERNATIVES

One alternative is bread from a local bakery. However, many bakers are using technology similar to CBP, which can render the bread rather tasteless, lightweight and insubstantial.

Organic bread is catching on. In London and the South East, Goswells produces organic bread on behalf of Doves Farm and Whole Earth Foods. In the North West there's Sakers and in the Gloucestershire region there's Hobbs House.

Good bread need contain only flour, yeast, water and salt.

- Authentic Bread
- Doves Farm
- Fine Lady
- Greggs
- Village Bakery
- Warburton's
- Whole Earth

- Allinson
- Burgen
- Kingsmill
- Rathbones
- Sunblest
- William Jackson

- Enjoy Organic
- Granary
- Hovis
- Mothers Pride
- Nimble

Brand Name	ENVIRONMENT				ANIMALS			PEOPLE				EXTRAS			Company group
	Environmental Reporting	Pollution	Nuclear Power	Other	Animal Testing	Factory Farming	Other Animal Rights	Oppressive Regimes	Workers' Rights	Irresponsible Marketing	Armaments	Genetic Engineering	Boycott Call	Political Donations	
Allinson	●	○	●	●	●	●	●	○	●	●	●	●	●		Wittington Investments
Authentic Bread	●	●	●	●	●	●	●	●	●	●	●	●	●		Authentic Bread Co Ltd
Burgen	●	○	●	●	●	●	●	○	●	●	●	●	●		Wittington Investments
Doves Farm	●	●	●	●	●	●	●	●	●	●	●	●	●		Doves Farm Foods
Enjoy Organic	●	●	○	●	●	○	●	○	●	●	●	○	●		Doughty Hanson
Fine Lady	●	●	●	●	●	●	○	●	●	●	●	●	●		Heygate & Sons
Granary	●	●	○	●	●	○	●	○	●	●	●	○	●		Doughty Hanson
Greggs	●	●	●	●	●	●	○	●	●	●	●	●	●		Greggs Plc
Hovis	●	●	○	●	●	○	●	○	●	●	●	○	●		Doughty Hanson
Kingsmill	●	○	●	●	●	●	●	○	●	●	●	●	●		Wittington Investments
Mother's Pride	●	●	○	●	●	○	●	○	●	●	●	○	●		Doughty Hanson
Nimble	●	●	○	●	●	○	●	○	●	●	●	○	●		Doughty Hanson
Rathbones	○	●	●	◉	●	●	●	●	●	●	●	○	●		Greencore Group
Sunblest	●	○	●	●	●	●	●	○	●	●	●	●	●		Wittington Investments
Village Bakery	●	●	●	●	●	●	●	●	●	●	●	●	●		The Village Bakery Melmerby
Warburtons	●	●	●	●	●	●	●	●	●	●	●	●	●		Warburtons Ltd
Whole Earth	●	●	●	●	●	●	●	●	●	●	●	●	●		Whole Earth Foods
William Jackson	●	●	●	●	○	○	●	○	●	●	●	●	●		William Jackson & Son Ltd

Key

- ● Top rating (no criticisms found)
- ○ Middle rating
- ● Bottom rating
- ◉ A related company has a bottom rating and the company itself has a middle rating
- ○ A related company has a middle rating
- ● A related company has a bottom rating

Source: ECRA-See page 14 for full key to symbols.

185

Cat & dog food

We tend to get rather limited choice with the cat and dog food we buy in the supermarkets, because they mainly sell products from only two manufacturers – Mars and Nestlé. Apart from trying to find the healthiest and most organic alternatives, perhaps we should also be more aware of the bigger issues like animal testing and vegetarianism for pets.

ORGANIC

Buying organic food is a way of avoiding factory-farmed meat, especially where a vegetarian diet is unsuitable. Some of the new organic brands are Yarrah and Pascoe's, both of which now sell in supermarkets.

We should always introduce new foods slowly to a pet, as they may not readily accept them at first. If it is possible feed pets home-cooked food although it is advisable to talk to a vet about this, as there is a risk of them developing imbalances in vitamins and minerals. Dogs need the right phosphorous/calcium ratio to maintain healthy bones. Without taurine, an amino acid that comes almost only from animal sources, cats can go blind. Feeding raw fish too often can cause neurological problems.

ANIMAL TESTING

The British Union for the Abolition of Vivisection (BUAV) has discovered bad cases of animal testing by the pet food industry. It was found in 2000 that all the major companies had authorised tests when developing new products. These included: Alpo Pet Foods (Nestlé), Pedigree (Mars), Hills Pet Nutrition (Colgate-Palmolive), Ralston Purina and Iams (Procter & Gamble). Procedures in the UK may involve some of the following: isolation of animals for long periods, endoscopy and tissue biopsy, frequent changes of diet which may cause digestive distress, regular sedations and anaesthetics, enemas, application of skin irritants and plucking of hairs from the base of the tail. Experiments in the US are likely to be even more invasive.

BUY THE DRIED STUFF

Some dried food formulations are thought to be healthier than tinned food. Pets need to eat more tinned food than dried to gain the same amount of nutrition.

The environmental evidence is also in favour of dried food. Tinned foods are at least 60 per cent water, making the transported volume and weight much greater. Paper bags are obviously a lower environmental impact choice than tins.

Bulk-buying is preferable, whether in the form of large sacks or tins.

The new innovation of single-serve portions in plastic pouches and foil trays is utterly wasteful of resources.

VEGETARIAN PETS?

It is highly controversial but some argue that dogs can be fed a vegan diet, and three companies at least make vegan and vegetarian dog food – Top Number Feeds (Happidog), Suma (Wackidog) and Vink Sales (Yarrah). Vink also makes meat and fish-based products.

Cats do need meat because they require taurine. If they are deprived of it they will soon turn to hunting birds and mice for meat. However, the Vegan Society imports something called Vegecat from the US, designed for adding to home-cooked cat food.

- Hi-Life
- Pascoe's
- Wackidog
  (dog food only)
- Wagg
  (dog food only)
- Webbox
  (dog food only)
- Yarrah

- Butchers
  (dog food only)
- Eukanuba
- Hills Science Diet
- Iams

- Bakers Complete
  (dog food only)
- Friskies
- Omega Complete
  (cat food only)
- Pedigree
  (dog food only)
- Spillers
- Whiskas (cat food only)

BRAND NAME	ENVIRONMENT				ANIMALS			PEOPLE				EXTRAS			Company group
	Environmental Reporting	Pollution	Nuclear Power	Other	Animal Testing	Factory Farming	Other Animal Rights	Oppressive Regimes	Workers' Rights	Irresponsible Marketing	Armaments	Genetic Engineering	Boycott Call	Political Donations	
CAT & DOG FOOD															
EUKANUBA	●	●	●	○	●	●	●	●	●	○	●	○	●		Procter & Gamble
FRISKIES	○	○	●	○	●	●	●	●	●	●	●	●	●		Nestlé SA
HI-LIFE	●	●	●	●	●	●	●	●	●	●	●	●	●		Town & Country Petfoods Ltd
HILLS SCIENCE DIET	○	●	●	●	●	●	●	●	○	●	●	●	●		Colgate-Palmolive
IAMS	●	●	●	○	●	●	●	●	●	○	●	○	●		Procter & Gamble
PASCOE'S	●	●	●	●	●	●	●	●	●	●	●	●	●		Primetime Petfoods Ltd
SPILLERS	○	○	●	○	●	●	●	●	●	●	●	●	●		Nestlé SA
YARRAH	●	●	●	●	●	●	○	●	●	●	●	●	●		Roelevink Beheer BV
CAT FOOD															
OMEGA COMPLETE	○	○	●	○	●	●	●	●	●	●	●	●	●		Nestlé SA
WHISKAS	●	○	●	●	●	●	●	●	●	○	●	○	●		Mars Inc
DOG FOOD															
BAKERS COMPLETE	○	○	●	○	●	●	●	●	●	●	●	●	●		Nestlé SA
BUTCHER'S	●	●	●	●	●	●	○	●	●	●	●	●	●		FW Baker Ltd
PEDIGREE	●	○	●	●	●	●	●	●	○	●	●	○	●		Mars Inc
WACKIDOG	●	●	●	●	●	●	●	●	●	●	●	●	●		Suma Wholefoods
WAGG	●	●	●	●	●	●	●	●	●	●	●	●	●		Wagg Foods
WEBBOX	●	●	●	●	●	●	●	●	●	●	●	●	●		Pet's Choice Ltd

Key

● Top rating (no criticisms found)

○ Middle rating

● Bottom rating

● A related company has a bottom rating and the company itself has a middle rating

○ A related company has a middle rating

● A related company has a bottom rating

Source: ECRA-See page 14 for full key to symbols.

Good Health
& Beauty

Eye care products

As spectacles and contact lenses become increasingly sophisticated they tend to use new materials that may have environmental impacts.

SPECTACLES

Chemicals are used to coat both contact lenses and spectacle lenses which may degrade into toxic materials when they are disposed of. However there are some more ecologically-aware companies attending to this problem by producing special lens coatings which degrade into harmless substances within seven days.

Many plastic spectacle lenses are made from 'CR39', a synthetic material that is kept in cold storage and cleaned with freon gas before coating. These may have an overall higher effect on the environment than glass lenses.

Frames with higher environmental impacts include those made of titanium or petroleum-based plastics.

The frames recommended by ECRA are those made from cellulose acetate, which are derived from plant cellulose and acetic acid, both of which are sustainable materials.

SCIENTIFIC AND MILITARY CONNECTIONS

Perhaps it's in the nature of precision engineering that some leading contact lens manufacturers are also involved in other activities which some of us may find distasteful – such as pursuing monopolies in human gene research or making accessories for the defence industry. Some of these involvements are shown on the table.

SOLUTION MYSTERIES

Although contact lens solutions may not appear to contain animal-derived ingredients, most brands are likely to have been tested on animals. The Vegan Society publishes a list of vegan-friendly contact lens solutions.

ALTERNATIVES

Laser treatment and the 'Bates method' of eyesight correction are possible alternatives to spectacles or contact lenses. Laser treatment is extremely expensive, however, while the Bates method – which involves exercises to retrain the eyes to relax and refocus – has not convinced a lot of people that it actually works!

Another 'ethical' idea is to buy a decent pair of spectacles to please oneself but make a donation to charities that provide opthalmic help to people in poor countries, such as Vision Aid Overseas.

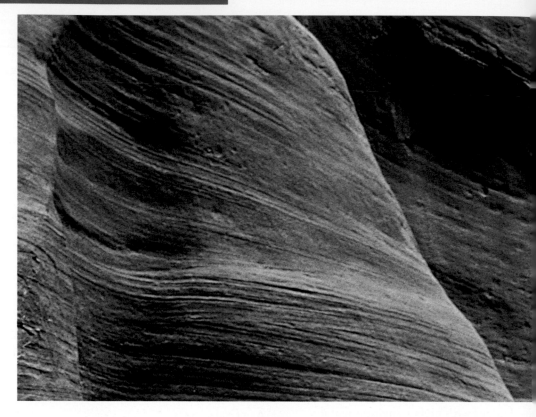

- Allergan
- Sauflon

- Bausch & Lomb
- Chauvin Pharm

- Alcon
- Cibavision
- Johnson & Johnson
- Pilkington Barnes - Hind
- Wesley- Jessen

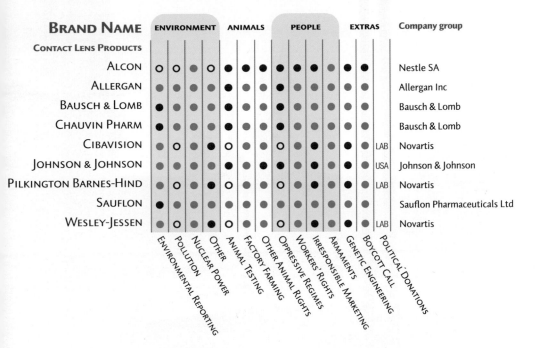

BRAND NAME — ENVIRONMENT | ANIMALS | PEOPLE | EXTRAS | Company group

CONTACT LENS PRODUCTS

Brand Name	Company group
ALCON	Nestle SA
ALLERGAN	Allergan Inc
BAUSCH & LOMB	Bausch & Lomb
CHAUVIN PHARM	Bausch & Lomb
CIBAVISION	Novartis
JOHNSON & JOHNSON	Johnson & Johnson
PILKINGTON BARNES-HIND	Novartis
SAUFLON	Sauflon Pharmaceuticals Ltd
WESLEY-JESSEN	Novartis

Column categories: ENVIRONMENTAL REPORTING · POLLUTION · NUCLEAR POWER · OTHER · ANIMAL TESTING · FACTORY FARMING · OTHER ANIMAL RIGHTS · OPPRESSIVE REGIMES · WORKERS' RIGHTS · IRRESPONSIBLE MARKETING · ARMAMENTS · GENETIC ENGINEERING · BOYCOTT CALL · POLITICAL DONATIONS

Key

● Top rating (no criticisms found)

○ Middle rating

● Bottom rating

◕ A related company has a bottom rating and the company itself has a middle rating

○ A related company has a middle rating

● A related company has a bottom rating

Source: ECRA-See page 14 for full key to symbols.

Perfumes & aftershaves

Perfumes make up one of the ultimate consumer luxuries. Driven by huge advertising campaigns and promotional activities, the fragrance industry is locked onto the 'aspirational' and escapist part of human nature.

SECRET INGREDIENTS

Apart from the dream and a briefly lingering scent, what we are really being sold in our bottle of perfume is nothing more than a container of unnamed and unspecified chemicals, or if we're lucky, a phial full of essential oils.

Perfume recipes have so far been protected from compulsory labelling as a result of highly-effective multinational company lobbying. Perfume was recently excluded from EU laws aimed at full ingredient listings because most perfumes had 'too many ingredients' to list. The cosmetics and toiletries industry has around 6,000–8,000 ingredients to play with, although it is hardly likely that any single perfume uses more than 20 or so of these. Only about half of the thousands of ingredients available are the fragrances themselves.

ALLERGIES & ANIMAL CRUELTY

Since a third of all allergies are caused by fragrance, the elixir in the bottle might give you headaches, rashes or make you sneeze.

In addition to fragrance, perfumes sometimes contain cruelly-derived ingredients and fixatives like musk ('a dried secretion from the preputial follicles of the musk deer'), civet (taken from the scent glands of the Ethiopian civet cat), ambergris (taken from sperm whales) and castor (from follicles near the genitals of beavers).

The perfume may also have been made from flowers picked in the Third World (where many of the cheaper essential oils are sourced), often using child labour.

Unfortunately, since the manufacturers are not obliged to list their ingredients, there is no easy way of finding out quite what your favourite perfume does contain.

TARGETING THE KIDS

Recently, child protection authorities and watchdog groups have criticised the perfume industry for the marketing of scents for children.

Since 1995, Versace, Agnes B, Nina Ricci, Givenchy and Guerlain have all introduced children's perfumes for children aged between 4 and 15.

Some watchdog groups have expressed the fear that the premature sexualisation of children in certain advertisements runs the risk of legitimising and encouraging sexual interest in children

WOMEN'S
- Amethyst Mist
- Aurelia
- Chanel Nº 5
- White Musk

MEN'S
- Activist
- Aurelius
- Ginger FM
- Sirius

WOMEN'S
- Beautiful
- Joop
- Opium
- Youth Dew

MEN'S
- Aramis
- Jazz

WOMEN'S
- Anais Anais
- Charlie
- CK One (Unisex)
- Dune

MEN'S
- Farenheit
- Lynx
- Old Spice
- Safari for Men

Brand Name	Environmental Reporting	Pollution	Nuclear Power	Other	Animal Testing	Factory Farming	Other Animal Rights	Oppressive Regimes	Workers' Rights	Irresponsible Marketing	Armaments	Genetic Engineering	Boycott Call	Political Donations		Company group
WOMEN'S																
Amethyst Mist	●	●	●	●	●	●	●	●	●	●	●	●	●	●		Dolma
Anais Anais	○	○	●	○	●	●	●	●	●	●	●	●	●	●		Gesparal/Nestlé
Aurelia	●	●	●	●	●	●	●	●	●	●	●	●	●	●		Fine Fragrances & Cosmetics
Beautiful	○	●	●	●	●	●	●	○	●	●	●	●	●	●	USA	Estee Lauder Cos
Chanel No 5	●	●	●	●	●	●	●	●	●	●	●	●	●	●		Pamerco
Charlie	●	●	●	○	●	●	●	●	●	●	●	●	●	●	USA	McAndrews & Forbes Holdings
CK One (Unisex)	●	●	●	●	●	●	●	●	●	○	●	○	●	●		Unilever
Dune	○	●	●	●	●	●	●	●	●	●	●	●	●	●		LVMH
Joop	○	●	●	○	●	●	●	●	●	○	●	●	●	●		Reckitt Benckiser
Opium	●	●	●	●	●	●	●	●	●	●	●	○	●	●		Gucci Group
White Musk	○	●	●	●	●	●	●	●	●	○	●	●	●	●		Body Shop
Youth Dew	○	●	●	●	●	●	●	○	●	●	●	●	●	●	USA	Estee Lauder Cos
MEN'S																
Activist	○	●	●	●	●	●	●	●	●	○	●	●	●	●		Body Shop
Aramis	○	●	●	●	●	●	●	○	●	●	●	●	●	●	USA	Estee Lauder Cos
Aurelius	●	●	●	●	●	●	●	●	●	●	●	●	●	●		Fine Fragrances & Cosmetics
Fahrenheit	○	●	●	●	●	●	●	●	●	●	●	●	●	●		LVMH
Jazz	●	●	●	●	●	●	●	●	●	●	●	○	●	●		Gucci Group
Lynx	●	●	●	●	●	●	●	●	●	○	●	○	●	●		Unilever
Old Spice	●	●	●	○	●	●	●	●	●	○	●	○	●	●		Procter & Gamble
Safari for Men	○	○	●	○	●	●	●	●	●	●	●	●	●	●		Gesparal/Nestlé
Sirius	●	●	●	●	●	●	●	●	●	●	●	●	●	●		Dolma

Column group headings: ENVIRONMENT | ANIMALS | PEOPLE | EXTRAS | Company group

Key

● Top rating (no criticisms found)

○ Middle rating

● Bottom rating

◐ A related company has a bottom rating and the company itself has a middle rating

○ A related company has a middle rating

● A related company has a bottom rating

Source: ECRA-See page 14 for full key to symbols.

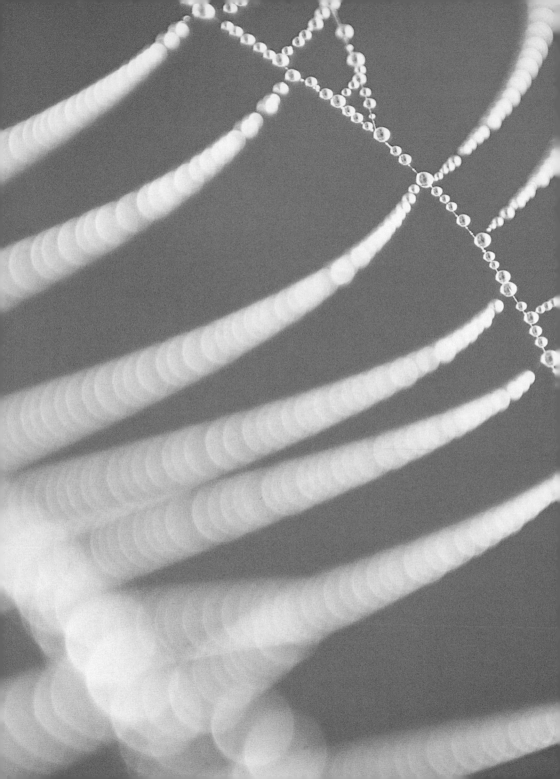

Sun Protectors

While we should all protect ourselves from sunburn, there is no need to spend massively on the most 'technologically advanced' products available. Some of the cheaper sunscreens work perfectly well.

PRODUCTS

Sun protection formulations come as creams, lotions, gels, oils, sprays and lipscreen. It is useful that most of these sun care products carry ingredients lists because there are certain substances we may wish to avoid for health reasons.

'Physical' sunblocks, which form a barrier to incoming light, are considered very safe and cause very few allergic reactions. They contain reflective particles, usually zinc oxide or titanium dioxide, which can now be made microfine but may still leave a white sheen on the skin. Physical sunblocks are often in cream form, good for people with oily skin and particularly water resistant.

More controversial are some of the agents in so-called 'chemical' sunscreens, which, rather than blocking it, react with ultra violet (UV) light to prevent it from damaging skin cells. Common active ingredients include para-amino benzoic acid (PABA), padimate-o, cinnamates and benzophenones. PABA and oxy- and dioxybenzone can sting already burned skin, and some people are allergic to them.

Chemical sunscreens, which are often absorbable lotions, should be applied at least 20 minutes before exposure to the sun, as it takes them that long to become effective. Light-absorbing chemicals are often inactivated by sunlight, so unless they are marked 'photostable', regular reapplication is especially important.

No sun protection product of any kind should be used on babies under six months, as their skin is not ready to deal with it.

UVA AND UVB

Sunscreens filter out ultra violet light. Both the UVA and UVB portions of the sun's light spectrum contribute to the 'photoaging' of the skin, and overexposure to both is thought to increase the risk of malignant melanoma, the most dangerous form of skin cancer.

The UVA safety rating is shown on most products by a line of four stars, underlined by 'low', 'high' or 'maximum'. Where the star symbols are absent, look for the words 'broad spectrum' to be sure of at least some UVA protection.

The Sun Protection Factor (SPF) relates to UVB, the wavelength which causes skin to redden. The SPF dictates how much longer a person can stay in the sun without burning than if they were unprotected: if you normally burn after 30 minutes, wearing Factor 6 would theoretically give you three hours' untroubled sunbathing. Note that very generous amounts of sunscreen are applied in the clinical trials, and being too sparing – or rubbing in opaque cream until it can't be seen – may drastically reduce the level of protection.

ALTERNATIVES

Regular and moderate unprotected exposure to the sun in the early morning or late afternoon can help maintain a protective tan (the rough equivalent of SPF 3) and will keep vitamin D at an optimum level. Wearing wide-brimmed hats and loose, protective clothing (black has the highest SPF) can also play a part in an overall 'safe sun' strategy. Hat brims should be at least 3 inches (8cm) all the way round. On hot days, even when wearing high factor sunscreen, it is wise to avoid direct sunlight between 11 a.m. and 3 p.m.

Remember that a history of painful or blistering sunburn during the first 10-20 years of life could double the risk of skin cancer later. Even people with dark skins should think about using sunscreen products.

AVOIDING SUNBURN

- Avoid most direct sunlight between 11 a.m and 3 p.m.
- When walking in the midday sun, wear a cap or wide-brimmed hat, and keep shoulders covered
- When buying skin protection, look for the best sun protection factor (SPF) and protection against ultraviolet A (UVA)
- If sunbathing, always apply the recommended level of protection

- Body Shop
- Clarins
- Delph
- Hawaiian Tropic
- Honesty
- Malibu
- NoAd
- Uvistat

- Banana Boat
- Calypso
- Elizabeth Arden
- Nivea Sun
- Solait

- Ambre Solaire
- Delial
- Johnson's Suncare
- Piz Buin
- Soltan

BRAND NAME	ENVIRONMENT				ANIMALS				PEOPLE				EXTRAS			Company group
	Environmental Reporting	Pollution	Nuclear Power	Other	Animal Testing	Animal Testing Policy	Factory Farming	Other Animal Rights	Oppressive Regimes	Workers' Rights	'Irresponsible' Marketing	Armaments	Genetic Engineering	Boycott Call	Political Donations	
AMBRE SOLAIRE																Gesparal/Nestlé
BANANA BOAT																Playtex Products Inc
BODY SHOP																Body Shop
CALYPSO																Linco Care
CLARINS																Clarins
DELIAL																Sara Lee
DELPH																Fenton Pharmaceuticals
ELIZABETH ARDEN																Elizabeth Arden Inc
HAWAIIAN TROPIC																Tanning Research Laboratories Ltd
HONESTY																Honesty Cosmetics
JOHNSON'S SUNCARE															USA	Johnson & Johnson
MALIBU																Malibu Health Products Inc
NIVEA SUN																Beiersdorf
NOAD																Richards & Appleby
PIZ BUIN															LAB	Novartis AG
SOLAIT																De Hoge Dennen Beheer
SOLTAN																Boots
UVISTAT																Eastern Pharmaceuticals

Key

- ● Top rating (no criticisms found)
- ○ Middle rating
- ● Bottom rating
- ◐ A related company has a bottom rating and the company itself has a middle rating
- ○ A related company has a middle rating
- ● A related company has a bottom rating

Source: ECRA-See page 14 for full key to symbols.

Soap

Few of us take much interest in the ingredients of the soap we use. A single bar may contain a variety, and perhaps we should consider whether they are really necessary. Natural and hand-made products are much more 'friendly'.

INGREDIENTS

Made from animal or vegetable fats, oils or grease, soap is formed when the fats interact with an alkali. Preservatives, salts, colours, perfumes, moisturisers and emulsifiers may then be added, with the more adventurous brands including fruits, spices and essential oils. Traditionally, soaps were produced from animal fats such as fish oils or tallow, listed in the ingredients as 'sodium tallowate'. The Vegan Society describes tallow as 'hard animal fat, especially that obtained from the parts about the kidneys of ruminating animals.' Although there are vegetable alternatives, many of the major soap brands still contain animal fats and consequently are not suitable for vegetarians or vegans.

Vegetable soaps may also contain added ingredients such as honey, lanolin and milk, preventing them from being suitable for vegans. Lush, Caurnie, Suma, Faith and Body Shop soaps are all suitable for vegetarians. Caurnie and Faith soaps are all vegan, while all except Suma's honey soaps are suitable for vegans. Body Shop produces a list of its 'vegan non-friendly' products and Lush soaps clearly labels those which are suitable for vegans.

MAKING SOAP CLEANLY

Most of the bigger brand soaps are made from a common soap bar, manufactured by large commercial producers who sell it on in the form of dried soap nodules to individual soap makers for reprocessing.

Soaps made by the 'alternative' producers, such as Caurnie, Faith and Suma are hand-made, which, if nothing else, keeps more people employed. According to information from Suma, the cold saponification process used by Suma and Caurnie is more energy-efficient as 'all the ingredients remain in the mix, with only such heat input as is required to raise the temperature of the mix to body heat.'

A commercial processor may use a boiling process which could consume up to 65kw hours of electricity and 15 tonnes of water in producing 1 tonne of soap. The alternative soap makers claim that commercial producers extract the glycerine, selling it as a by-product, instead of leaving it in the soap. Since glycerine is a natural moisturiser, it explains why many soaps can dry the skin.

SYNTHETICS AND PACKAGING

Most of the major soaps contain synthetic (petrochemical-based) ingredients, while Suma, Faith and Caurnie use natural ingredients and instead of adding an artificial fragrance use essential oils or fruits to scent their soaps. The synthetic ingredients used by the larger companies are often irritants for sensitive skin.

The packaging by the major brands is often excessive, with Imperial Leather – the UK's best-selling soap – using three wrappers, including a box. In comparison, Suma's soap is sold completely loose and just wrapped in a brown envelope. Lush products also have little or no packaging and Faith and Caurnie soaps also have minimal packaging.

Those small bits of soap that are too small to wash with can be kept in a soap jar which can be used in hot water as a soft jelly to use for washing-up.

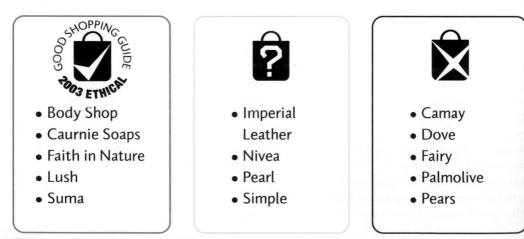

- Body Shop
- Caurnie Soaps
- Faith in Nature
- Lush
- Suma

- Imperial Leather
- Nivea
- Pearl
- Simple

- Camay
- Dove
- Fairy
- Palmolive
- Pears

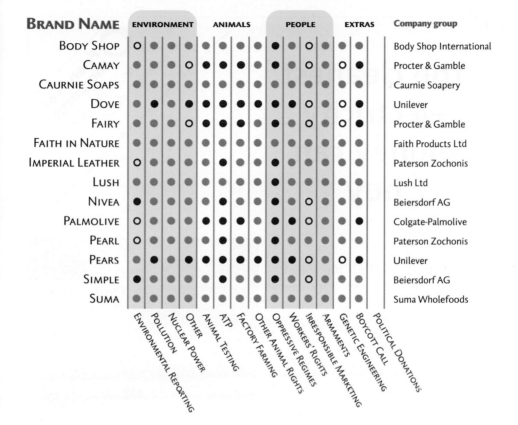

BRAND NAME	ENVIRONMENT	ANIMALS	PEOPLE	EXTRAS	Company group
BODY SHOP					Body Shop International
CAMAY					Procter & Gamble
CAURNIE SOAPS					Caurnie Soapery
DOVE					Unilever
FAIRY					Procter & Gamble
FAITH IN NATURE					Faith Products Ltd
IMPERIAL LEATHER					Paterson Zochonis
LUSH					Lush Ltd
NIVEA					Beiersdorf AG
PALMOLIVE					Colgate-Palmolive
PEARL					Paterson Zochonis
PEARS					Unilever
SIMPLE					Beiersdorf AG
SUMA					Suma Wholefoods

Column categories (angled labels): ENVIRONMENTAL REPORTING, POLLUTION, NUCLEAR POWER, OTHER, ANIMAL TESTING, ATP, FACTORY FARMING, OTHER ANIMAL RIGHTS, OPPRESSIVE REGIMES, WORKERS' RIGHTS, IRRESPONSIBLE MARKETING, ARMAMENTS, GENETIC ENGINEERING, BOYCOTT CALL, POLITICAL DONATIONS

Key

● Top rating (no criticisms found)

○ Middle rating

● Bottom rating

◉ A related company has a bottom rating and the
company itself has a middle rating

○ A related company has a middle rating

● A related company has a bottom rating

Source: ECRA-See page 14 for full key to symbols.

Shampoo

Hair care is intrinsic to our desire to present a pleasing image in the increasingly fashion-conscious world we live in. Even those with a concern for nature and the environment can be seduced by the apparently 'natural' or even 'organic' kinds of shampoo and conditioner that now litter the shelves of supermarkets and chemists' stores.

THE NATURAL LOOK

Over the past few years, booming interest in organic produce has caused the mainstream cosmetic companies to flirt heavily, and successfully, with the natural image in launching their new product lines. This corporate romance with nature can be criticised as a cheap attempt to appear ecologically sound, as the few token 'natural' ingredients invariably mask the usual chemical cocktail. Alternative groups, including ECRA, have called for Elida Fabergé to withdraw or rename its Organics line until all ingredients are certified organic. Of course, alternative producers have long been proclaiming the benefits of natural ingredients, with product lines true to their principles.

SUDS LAW

The long list of ingredients on the back of a shampoo bottle can be hard to decipher without specialist chemical knowledge. A commonly-used shampoo ingredient due to its propensity to foam is Sodium Laurel Sulphate, or its milder form Sodium Laureth Sulphate. Claims about the former's damaging health effects point to it being an allergen, with symptoms including skin and eye irritation. Industry replies to such concerns emphasise that these chemicals are used in measured amounts that have been legally decreed as safe for use.

Dandruff is a problem that many people are tackling with medicated shampoos. Anti-dandruff shampoos again can contain potentially toxic chemicals and can even aggravate the problem. Eating foods that contain the right fats – such as raw nuts and cold-pressed vegetable oils – is one way to address the imbalance.

ALTERNATIVES

In the days before shampoo, people resorted to more imaginative methods of achieving glossy locks. Soap was used as an all-round cleanser for hair and body, but as water has become more alkaline (hard) its effectiveness has declined, leaving hair rough and tangled. In areas with a soft water supply, using a plain soap with conditioner is an option. Otherwise adding something acidic along with soap, such as vinegar or lemon juice, can neutralise the hard water. If you follow up with conditioner, your hair should be left healthy. It is possible to dispense with shampoo completely. However, people may find the transitional period unpleasant as the scalp's naturally-produced oils (washed out by shampooing) kick back into action.

ANIMAL TESTING

Some companies skirt round the issue of animal testing, at the same time keeping themselves open to new ingredients, by adhering to the 'five-year rolling rule' which means five years must have elapsed since the ingredient was tested on animals. Naturewatch and BUAV support use of the 'fixed cut off date', whereby companies refuse to use ingredients tested on animals after a certain date. In the table, a full red circle indicates the company has no written animal testing policy statement, or did not

reply to ECRA's request for one, or sent a policy with standards less stringent than those required for an empty red circle (middle rating). An empty red circle indicates that the company does not have a fixed cut-off date, but has a policy of not testing products or ingredients on animals, and of not commissioning such tests. A green circle indicates that the company does not sell animal tested products or ingredients, and upholds a fixed cut-off date. (For details as to which companies did and did not provide animal testing policy statements, please see the relevant ECRA Research Supplement).

- Body shop
- Faith in Nature
- Honesty
- Weleda
- Neem Care
- Original Source

- Superdrug
- Henara
- VO5
- Botanics

- Head & Shoulders
- Pantene Pro-V
- Aussie
- Organics
- L'Oreal

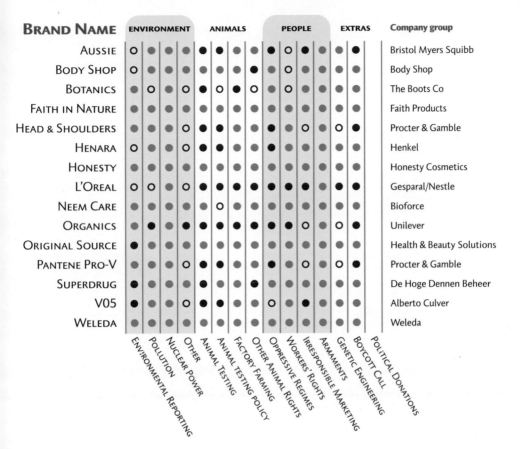

BRAND NAME	ENVIRONMENT	ANIMALS	PEOPLE	EXTRAS	Company group
AUSSIE					Bristol Myers Squibb
BODY SHOP					Body Shop
BOTANICS					The Boots Co
FAITH IN NATURE					Faith Products
HEAD & SHOULDERS					Procter & Gamble
HENARA					Henkel
HONESTY					Honesty Cosmetics
L'OREAL					Gesparal/Nestle
NEEM CARE					Bioforce
ORGANICS					Unilever
ORIGINAL SOURCE					Health & Beauty Solutions
PANTENE PRO-V					Procter & Gamble
SUPERDRUG					De Hoge Dennen Beheer
V05					Alberto Culver
WELEDA					Weleda

Column headings: Environmental Reporting, Pollution, Nuclear Power, Other, Animal Testing, Animal Testing Policy, Factory Farming, Other Animal Rights, Oppressive Regimes, Workers' Rights, Irresponsible Marketing, Armaments, Genetic Engineering, Boycott Call, Political Donations

Key

- ● Top rating (no criticisms found)
- ○ Middle rating
- ● Bottom rating
- ◓ A related company has a bottom rating and the company itself has a middle rating
- ○ A related company has a middle rating
- ● A related company has a bottom rating

Source: ECRA–See page 14 for full key to symbols.

Essential oils

The market for essential oils for personal relaxation and healing has grown rapidly in the last ten years. About 400 different kinds of essential oil are now available, each claims its own special fragrance and restorative or healing power. Before we start to use any oils, however, it is always good idea to get some guidance on the best uses for them and to know about some of the potential hazards of misuse. Because there are so many different brands of oils – with many of them distributed only through local networks – here we concentrate on the most common brand names.

ANCIENT REMEDIES

Aromatherapy as we know it today was rediscovered and researched in the 1930s but some forms of it are as old as humanity itself. Tea-tree, for example, has long been used as an antiseptic by the Aboriginal people of Australia. In ancient Egypt, priestesses were said to have burned oils and gums, such as frankincense, to clear their minds. The ancient cultures using aromatherapy included those of Egypt, Greece, Rome, Arabia, India and China. Rosemary was revered in several cultures as regenerative, which is probably why traces of the herb have been found in Egyptian tombs. In fourteenth-century England, pomanders of oranges and cloves were used (presumably unsuccessfully) to ward off the Black Death.

MIND AND BODY

Essential oils are usually used in the bath or in fragrancers (oil burners) or are blended with a carrier oil to produce a massage oil. Research into the oils – which can be extracted from herbs, spices, wood and flowers – suggests that they work on both the mental and physical levels. They are popular both for relieving stress and for helping to heal muscular, circulatory, respiratory, digestive and skin problems and disorders.

Most oils are obtained by distillation, whereby the plant material is placed in large vats and processed using steam, so that the cooled water can then be separated from the essential oil. No waste products occur, as both the oil and water can be used. Another process for producing essential oils is called 'expression'. (Essential oils should not be confused with those simply called 'aromatherapy oils', which are often a blend of oils and dilutants.)

TAKING CARE

As all essential oils are extremely concentrated, they should be kept away from the eyes, they should not be taken internally, they should not be applied on the skin undiluted and the dilution should be done following the instructions carefully. All bottles should have leaflets with appropriate safety warnings and clear instructions on use. The Aromatherapy Trade Council (ATC), the main representative body issues guidelines on responsible marketing, product labelling and marketing. Leading members of the ATC are Tisserand, Nelson & Russell, Essentially Oils, Neal's Yard and Gerard House.

There is a growing range of organic oils guaranteeing that pesticides have not been used on the plants from which they are extracted.

GOOD SHOPPING GUIDE 2003 ETHICAL
- Body Shop
- Culpeper
- Neal's Yard
- Nelson & Russell

- Tisserand
- Essentially Oils

- Nature's Garden
  (Holland & Barrett)
- Gerard House
- Boots

Brand Name	Environment				Animals			People				Extras			Company group
	Environmental Reporting	Pollution	Nuclear Power	Other	Animal Testing	Factory Farming	Other Animal Rights	Oppressive Regimes	Workers' Rights	Irresponsible Marketing	Armaments	Genetic Engineering	Boycott Call	Political Donations	
Body Shop	○	●	●	●	●	●	●	●	●	○	●	●	●	●	Body Shop
Boots	●	○	●	○	●	○	●	○	●	○	●	●	●	●	Boots
Culpeper	●	●	●	●	●	●	●	●	●	●	●	●	●	●	Culpeper
Essentially Oils	●	●	●	●	●	●	●	●	●	○	●	●	●	●	Essentially Oils Ltd
Gerard House	●	●	●	●	●	●	○	●	●	○	●	●	●	●	Peter Black Holdings Ltd
Nature's Garden (Holland & Barret)	●	●	●	●	●	●	●	●	●	○	●	●	●	●	NBTY
Neal's Yard	●	●	●	●	●	●	●	●	●	●	●	●	●	●	Neal's Yard Remedies
Nelson & Russell	●	●	●	●	●	●	●	●	●	●	●	●	●	●	A Nelson & Co Ltd
Tisserand	●	●	●	●	●	●	●	●	●	●	●	●	●	●	Aromatherapy Products Ltd

Key

- ● Top rating (no criticisms found)
- ○ Middle rating
- ● Bottom rating
- ● A related company has a bottom rating and the company itself has a middle rating
- ○ A related company has a middle rating
- ● A related company has a bottom rating

Source: ECRA-See page 14 for full key to symbols.

Care for others as you care for yourself

Viridian is a new kind of vitamin company dedicated to ethical business practices including environmental awareness, pure ingredients and charity donation.

In fact, in 2001/2002, Viridian is donating £30,000 to a range of environmental, children's and other selected charities including *NSPCC, Friends of the Earth, Childline, Woodland Trust, Shelter, The Orangutan Foundation, Help the Aged, Amnesty International, Terrence Higgins Trust, Barnados, National Deaf Children's Society, RSPB, Trees For London, UNICEF, Hackney City Farm, Born Free Foundation* and *Maggie's Cancer Care.*

Viridian supplies specialist health food stores and each year the stores vote which charities will benefit the following year – as the company grows, so do the charity donations.

Viridian vitamins and herbs are excellent quality and cost no more than comparable, non-donating brands found in the mass market. So, by switching to Viridian, you not only get the best in nutrition, you also help generate thousands for charities. Everyone's taking vitamins these days and what better way to take them than with a large dose of Viridian's feel-good factor.

The Viridian range of vitamins, minerals, herbs, amino acids and nutritional oils is available from selected independent health food stores.

viridian
Care for others as you care for yourself

For your nearest stockist call 01327 878050.
www.viridian-nutrition.com

Vitamins

Vitamin supplement pills have become popular as a way of boosting diets or fighting off infections, but most of the accompanying marketing is just a load of hype. The makers are keen to prey on our insecurities about inadequate diets. Healthy eating is definitely the best way to get all the vitamins we need, but if we are simply too busy to eat well then we may need the occasional pill to boost the system!

GOOD IN THEIR WAY

Vitamins are chemically-produced pills, and debates have arisen whether they are effective or not. A leading official of the Food Commission has argued that they are oversold and has expressed concerns over the health claims of many of the vitamins. So far, most research into vitamins has focused on the effects of vitamins in food, rather than those in pills. In Toronto, scientists found that carotenoids and nutrients such as vitamin E are 'more beneficial if eaten in foods rather than taken as supplements.' The micro-nutrients in food may also 'play an important role in the prevention of disease' and may not be found in pills or capsules.

One of the most convincing justifications for taking vitamin pills is that our busy lifestyles and the abundance of low-nutrient convenience foods mean that vitamin and mineral tablets may be needed to supplement a less-than-ideal diet. Pre-pregnant, or pregnant women are also advised to take folic acid supplements.

Research shows that people who take vitamins are in fact those who are less likely to need them, and that they already eat healthily. Advertisements and health editorials commonly target vegetarians and vegans as those who are most in need of supplements. However, both the Vegan and Vegetarian Societies argue that a healthy, mixed diet should provide us with all the nutrients we need.

INGREDIENTS

When the Food Commission conducted a survey into additives it was shocked by the numbers contained in supplements, as well as by the lack of clear labelling of ingredients. Its survey found a colouring in Redoxon which is banned in virtually all foods. Artificial sweeteners, aspartame and sorbitol, as well as talcum powder, silicon dioxide and anti-caking agents were found in some other supplements. More worryingly, a government survey in 1998 discovered higher-than-permitted levels of lead and arsenic in a number of supplements. Although the government did not at the time conclude that the products posed a significant risk, manufacturers were required to change formulations.

COMPANIES

At the time of our research, American Home Products (AHP) owned Solgar, one of the major vitamin brands. AHP and Numico have each been criticised by UNICEF for violating the WHO Code of Marketing, relating to the marketing of breast milk substitutes. (See ECRA background materials for more details).

PACKAGING

Many vitamin pills are vastly overpackaged. Some products – such as Seven Seas – are packaged in an outer box as well as the vitamin bottle, while Perfectil vitamins go even further by packaging each individual pill in its own bubble pack. The majority of vitamin bottles are also made from plastic, although a few brands use glass. Viridian was the only company offering recycling of

its bottles. Consumers can return their empty Viridian glass bottle to the place of purchase, receive a 25p refund, and the bottle gets recycled.

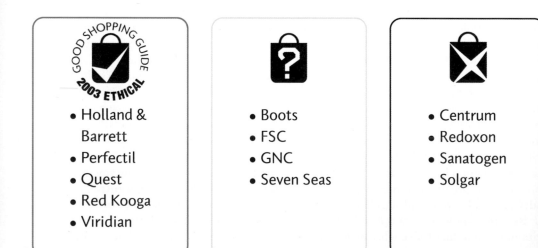

- Holland & Barrett
- Perfectil
- Quest
- Red Kooga
- Viridian

- Boots
- FSC
- GNC
- Seven Seas

- Centrum
- Redoxon
- Sanatogen
- Solgar

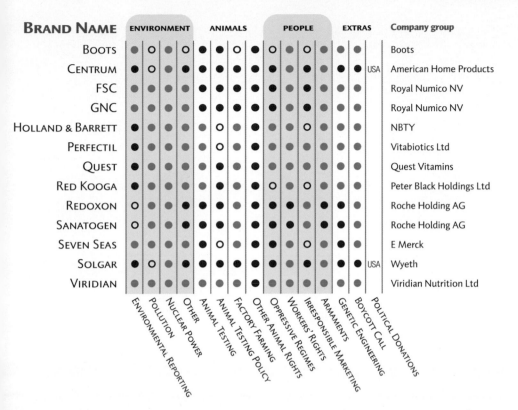

BRAND NAME	ENVIRONMENT	ANIMALS	PEOPLE	EXTRAS	Company group
BOOTS					Boots
CENTRUM				USA	American Home Products
FSC					Royal Numico NV
GNC					Royal Numico NV
HOLLAND & BARRETT					NBTY
PERFECTIL					Vitabiotics Ltd
QUEST					Quest Vitamins
RED KOOGA					Peter Black Holdings Ltd
REDOXON					Roche Holding AG
SANATOGEN					Roche Holding AG
SEVEN SEAS					E Merck
SOLGAR				USA	Wyeth
VIRIDIAN					Viridian Nutrition Ltd

Column headings: ENVIRONMENTAL REPORTING, POLLUTION, NUCLEAR POWER, OTHER, ANIMAL TESTING, ANIMAL TESTING POLICY, FACTORY FARMING, OTHER ANIMAL RIGHTS, OPPRESSIVE REGIMES, WORKERS' RIGHTS, IRRESPONSIBLE MARKETING, ARMAMENTS, GENETIC ENGINEERING, BOYCOTT CALL, POLITICAL DONATIONS

Key

● Top rating (no criticisms found)

O Middle rating

● Bottom rating

◐ A related company has a bottom rating and the
company itself has a middle rating

○ A related company has a middle rating

● A related company has a bottom rating

Source: ECRA-See page 14 for full key to symbols.

Pain remedies

Most of us do not bother our doctors when we suffer from headaches and instead look for a painkiller or analgesic such as paracetamol, aspirin or ibuprofen. Ethics may not be top of your list when you reach for emergency pain relief, but ethical alternatives *are* available.

BRANDS AND GENERICS

Like nearly every other consumer product, there is an abundance of different pain remedy brands available, with a choice of between 30 and 50 different analgesics in the shops. The main active ingredients are paracetamol (acetaminophen in the US), aspirin and ibuprofen.

Formulations may contain one of these or a combination and may also include codeine and other ingredients, such as caffeine. There are more brands available than there are formulations, many being identical but for the brand name. Branded painkillers are a good income for the pharmaceutical companies, as simply by branding a well-established drug – such as aspirin – they can sell it at an inflated price, sometimes as much as six times the price of a 'generic' (the term referring to the scientific name for a drug such as aspirin). Only drugs for which the patent has expired are available as generics and may be produced by any company. For example, since January 1998, it has been possible to purchase ibuprofen, whereas before this it was only available as a brand such as Nurofen. Painkillers come in a range of formats – capsules, tablets, caplets and soluble tablets. Vegetarians would probably do better to avoid capsules as they often contain gelatine.

ANIMAL TESTING

Most of the companies included in this report were known to be involved in animal testing. Although companies are obliged in most countries to test pharmaceutical products on animals, some are involved in testing not for medical use. Companies producing generics may be less likely to be involved in animal testing as they simply produce drugs that were developed by others.

ALTERNATIVES

Dealing with the causes of stress is usually preferable to having to deal with the symptoms such as pain. Regular exercise and relaxation techniques like yoga, meditation and massage can be good stress-busters. Aromatherapy can also be useful, and lavender is often recommended.

It has been suggested that migraines may be triggered by certain food and drink. The most common triggers are thought to be red wine, chocolate, cheese and citrus fruit. Avoiding these may limit the chances of an attack.

GOOD SHOPPING GUIDE
2003 ETHICAL

- Codis
- Disprin
- Disprol
- Lloyds Pharmacy
- Superdrug

- Aspro Clear
- Boots
- Feminax
- Neurofen
- Veganin

- Anadin
- Hedex
- Panadol
- Solpadeine

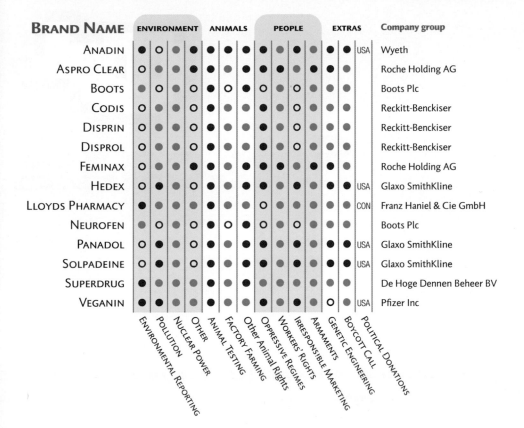

BRAND NAME	ENVIRONMENT				ANIMALS			PEOPLE				EXTRAS			Company group
ANADIN														USA	Wyeth
ASPRO CLEAR															Roche Holding AG
BOOTS															Boots Plc
CODIS															Reckitt-Benckiser
DISPRIN															Reckitt-Benckiser
DISPROL															Reckitt-Benckiser
FEMINAX															Roche Holding AG
HEDEX														USA	Glaxo SmithKline
LLOYDS PHARMACY														CON	Franz Haniel & Cie GmbH
NEUROFEN															Boots Plc
PANADOL														USA	Glaxo SmithKline
SOLPADEINE														USA	Glaxo SmithKline
SUPERDRUG															De Hoge Dennen Beheer BV
VEGANIN														USA	Pfizer Inc

Column categories (diagonal labels):
ENVIRONMENTAL REPORTING, POLLUTION, NUCLEAR POWER, OTHER, ANIMAL TESTING, FACTORY FARMING, Other Animal Rights, OPPRESSIVE REGIMES, WORKERS' RIGHTS, IRRESPONSIBLE MARKETING, ARMAMENTS, GENETIC ENGINEERING, BOYCOTT CALL, POLITICAL DONATIONS

Key

- ● Top rating (no criticisms found)
- ○ Middle rating
- ● Bottom rating
- ◉ A related company has a bottom rating and the company itself has a middle rating
- ○ A related company has a middle rating
- ● A related company has a bottom rating

Source: ECRA-See page 14 for full key to symbols.

fish.co.uk

Change your world.
Start here.

With your free ISP, helping people in need has never been easier. Make a difference...

...while you surf
100 per cent of the profits go to Christian Aid

...when you search
2p goes to Christian Aid every time you search the web

...when you shop
Top shops will donate up to 10 per cent when you shop online

Cold remedies

Cold remedies don't attempt to cure a cold but instead contain a combination of ingredients that target individual symptoms. There are more than 200 different cough and cold remedies and new or updated products are coming out all the time. This ethical report just looks at the cold remedies, rather than the cough medicines or decongestants for hay fever.

ATISHOO, ATISHOO, WE ALL FALL DOWN

The common cold is one of the most widespread infections, and it is caused by one of over 2,000 different viruses. Most of us suffer at least one cold a year. Instead of going to the doctor we seek out remedies at the chemists, where they are available without a prescription. Ingredients found amongst the most popular cold remedies often include a painkiller with a decongestant and caffeine.

BIG PHARMA

The companies in the cold remedy business are mostly big players in the pharmaceutical industry. It is an industry often and rightly criticised for inflated prices, animal testing and the marketing of banned or less suitable drugs in the Third World.

The Consumer Association has complained that branded cough and cold remedies are sold at higher prices than the equivalent generic drug. Some researchers have claimed that the remedies have no strictly medical benefit.

ANIMALS

According to UK law, a variety of medical experiments are specifically required before a pharmaceutical product can be licensed. Consequently almost all pharmaceutical companies conduct or fund a large proportion of animal experimentation. It is not just pharmaceutical products that are tested on animals. Companies such as Procter & Gamble are known to test cosmetic ingredients on animals, which is not a process required by law.

The arguments against animal testing of pharmaceuticals have been well documented. With the advent of new technologies, the alternatives to animal testing are also growing and include using tissue culture and computer modelling. Although testing may be required by law, and laws are made to regulate these practices, often animals have been found in appalling conditions.

ALTERNATIVES

A weak immune system will increase susceptibility to colds and other viruses. A balanced diet, including lots of fresh vegetables and fruit, will help maintain a healthy immune system. Garlic, echinacea and vitamin C are all popular cold-prevention measures. High stress levels have also been shown to weaken the immune system.

The best treatment of cold symptoms is a combination of painkillers and hot drinks with honey and lemon. Steam inhalations with oil vapour such as menthol or eucalyptus can be as effective as branded decongestants. Another popular remedy is to bathe with drops of lavender, tea-tree and eucalyptus essential oils.

- Cold-eeze
- Coldenza
- Olbas Oil

- Benylin 4 Flu
- Karvol
- Lemsip Original
- Nurofen Cold & Flu
- Sudafed

- Beecham's
- Day Nurse
- Vick's Vapour Rub

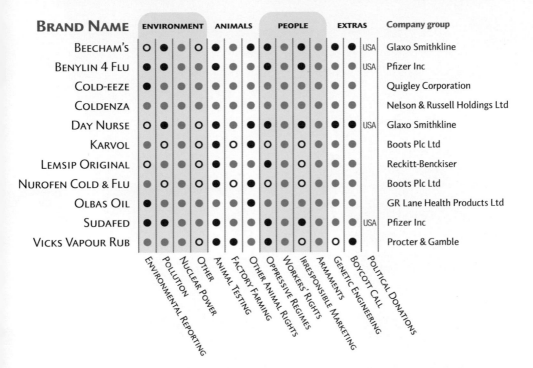

BRAND NAME	ENVIRONMENT	ANIMALS	PEOPLE	EXTRAS	Company group
Beecham's				USA	Glaxo Smithkline
Benylin 4 Flu				USA	Pfizer Inc
Cold-eeze					Quigley Corporation
Coldenza					Nelson & Russell Holdings Ltd
Day Nurse				USA	Glaxo Smithkline
Karvol					Boots Plc Ltd
Lemsip Original					Reckitt-Benckiser
Nurofen Cold & Flu					Boots Plc Ltd
Olbas Oil					GR Lane Health Products Ltd
Sudafed				USA	Pfizer Inc
Vicks Vapour Rub					Procter & Gamble

Column categories (diagonal labels):
ENVIRONMENTAL REPORTING · POLLUTION · NUCLEAR POWER · OTHER · ANIMAL TESTING · FACTORY FARMING · OTHER ANIMAL RIGHTS · OPPRESSIVE REGIMES · WORKERS' RIGHTS · IRRESPONSIBLE MARKETING · ARMAMENTS · GENETIC ENGINEERING · BOYCOTT CALL · POLITICAL DONATIONS

Key

● Top rating (no criticisms found)

O Middle rating

● Bottom rating

◒ A related company has a bottom rating and the company itself has a middle rating

○ A related company has a middle rating

● A related company has a bottom rating

Source: ECRA-See page 14 for full key to symbols.

Toothpaste

It's much more important for us to clean our teeth for the sake of our dental health than for cosmetic reasons. This is why we should hesitate before buying whitening and smokers' toothpastes, as these often contain abrasives. There are plenty of kinds to choose from with all the necessary information on ingredients to help us avoid those things that we don't really want to put in our mouths. This report covers the nine biggest manufacturers and seven alternative brands.

LABELLING

The British Dental Health Foundation and the British Dental Association both run labelling schemes which allow oral health and hygiene products to carry the BDHF or BDA logo. Companies have to pay for the initial checks on the products and then pay an annual fee to the relevant body in order to carry the logo. The Consumers' Association has concerns over accreditation schemes arguing that toothpastes without a logo are not necessarily any worse.

FLUORIDE

Some claim that fluoride is necessary for healthy teeth and that tooth decay rates have fallen by 75 per cent since fluoride toothpaste came onto the market in the 1970s. Concerns exist about adding fluoride to water supplies, and readers wishing to know more about this debate can contact: Safe Water Information Service, Eye Manor Cottage, Eye, Leominster HR6 0DT (*http://members.aol.com/forgood/swis/*). Readers worried about this issue can choose fluoride-free toothpastes such as Green People, Kingfisher, Tom's of Maine or the appropriate Weleda brand.

OTHER INGREDIENTS

Many toothpastes contain sodium lauryl sulphate (SLS), a synthetic foaming agent. Some experts have raised concerns about this ingredient, saying that it is a suspected gastro-intestinal or liver toxicant. Other concerns point to the fact that it has been associated with recurrent mouth ulcers. It is nevertheless an industrial-strength detergent, so many people may want to think twice before putting it in their mouths. However a small application for a short period followed by a thorough rinsing should be harmless for most people. For those with a recurring mouth ulcer problem, Green People and Weleda toothpastes are SLS-free.

Triclosan (which may also be listed under CH 3635, Irgasan Ch 3635 or Ster-Zac) is an antibacterial agent which has also been controversial because it may increase the groth of superbugs. It has not been shown to be dangerous for human health however.

All toothpastes list the active ingredients, so amounts of triclosan and fluoride salts present in the paste should always be found on the packet. Toothpaste brands which contain triclosan include Colgate, Crest, Mentadent P, Sensodyne F and Macleans. Other brands marketing themselves as 'antibacterial' may also contain triclosan.

PACKAGING

Most toothpastes now come in plastic tubes, and several in pump dispensers.

Some still come in the traditional aluminium tube. Tom's of Maine says that its aluminium tube, lined with food-grade plastic, can be recycled along with aluminium cans. Kingfisher Natural Toothpaste is packed in boxes manufactured from recycled cardboard and its tubes are made from biodegradable cellulose.

ALTERNATIVES

Dabur is an ayurvedic brand and made according to ancient Hindu principles.

If you wish to join the six per cent of the population who don't use toothpaste at all, experiment with sea salt, soot, chalk or bicarbonate of soda. The flavour of these can always be improved by adding a bit of mint essential oil.

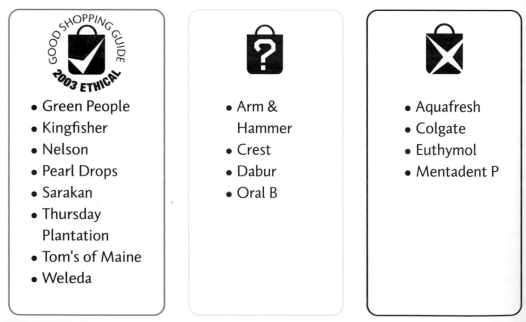

GOOD SHOPPING GUIDE 2003 ETHICAL	?	✗
• Green People	• Arm & Hammer	• Aquafresh
• Kingfisher	• Crest	• Colgate
• Nelson	• Dabur	• Euthymol
• Pearl Drops	• Oral B	• Mentadent P
• Sarakan		
• Thursday Plantation		
• Tom's of Maine		
• Weleda		

TOOTHPASTE

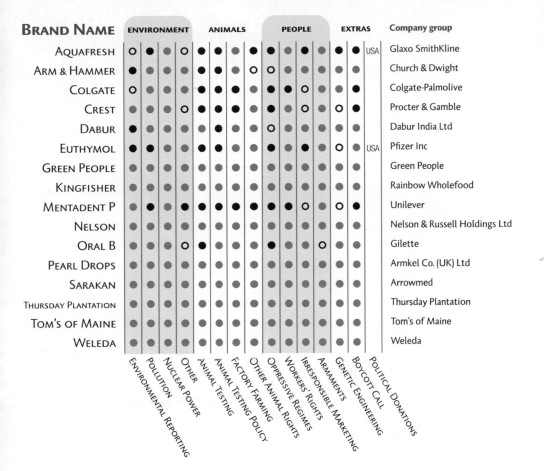

BRAND NAME	ENVIRONMENT	ANIMALS	PEOPLE	EXTRAS	Company group
AQUAFRESH				USA	Glaxo SmithKline
ARM & HAMMER					Church & Dwight
COLGATE					Colgate-Palmolive
CREST					Procter & Gamble
DABUR					Dabur India Ltd
EUTHYMOL				USA	Pfizer Inc
GREEN PEOPLE					Green People
KINGFISHER					Rainbow Wholefood
MENTADENT P					Unilever
NELSON					Nelson & Russell Holdings Ltd
ORAL B					Gilette
PEARL DROPS					Armkel Co. (UK) Ltd
SARAKAN					Arrowmed
THURSDAY PLANTATION					Thursday Plantation
TOM'S OF MAINE					Tom's of Maine
WELEDA					Weleda

Column headings:
ENVIRONMENTAL REPORTING · POLLUTION · NUCLEAR POWER · OTHER · ANIMAL TESTING · ANIMAL TESTING POLICY · FACTORY FARMING · OTHER ANIMAL RIGHTS · OPPRESSIVE REGIMES · WORKERS' RIGHTS · IRRESPONSIBLE MARKETING · ARMAMENTS · GENETIC ENGINEERING · BOYCOTT CALL · POLITICAL DONATIONS

Key

- ● Top rating (no criticisms found)
- O Middle rating
- ● Bottom rating
- ◉ A related company has a bottom rating and the company itself has a middle rating
- O A related company has a middle rating
- ● A related company has a bottom rating

Source: ECRA-See page 14 for full key to symbols.

Sanitary protection

Women in the UK typically spend more than £300 a year on sanitary protection, mostly on the Always, Allday and Tampax brands, which are all produced by one company, Procter & Gamble. They have been able to cash in on the fact that girls now start to menstruate much earlier than they used to (typically at between 10 and 13 years old). A new high-growth area is 'every-day panty liners', which have controversially been touted as intrinsic to 'daily freshness'. There are important health and environmental issues to consider, but alternatives are available.

HEALTH

Manufacturers estimate that ten per cent of women have permanently deserted the tampon due to fears of the blood infection Toxic Shock Syndrome (TSS). This is a rare, but painful and occasionally fatal, disease. Ninety-nine per cent of TSS cases are found in women wearing rayon-blend tampons, the most common kind. Natracare does 100 per cent cotton tampons, which may therefore be safer.

The superabsorbent polyacrylate gel AGM was banned from tampons in 1995 because of links to TSS, but it is still used in some towels. The main safety issue arises from the temptation to change gel-filled towels less frequently, causing a build up of bacteria. Additionally, a recent Canadian study on babies' nappies also found that when dry, AGM powder can travel up the urethra to the kidneys and cause scarring.

Women's Environmental Network (WEN) has campaigned on the issue of GM cotton in tampons and towels. Aside from the environmental objections to modification of the cotton crop, the organisation is concerned about potential alterations in absorbency levels increasing the risk of TSS, and about the potential transfer of antibiotic resistance marker genes. Using disposable sanitary products risks putting toxins next to your skin or vaginal tissue. Some residues, such as pesticides and dioxins from the bleaching process, have been linked to birth defects, reproductive disorders, depressed immunity and cancer.

THE ENVIRONMENT

Casual flushing of sanitary protection waste means that much of it ends up in rivers and sewage outfills, acting as a breeding ground for diseases and potentially being mistaken by sea mammals for prey. Otherwise, it festers in landfill sites, where it takes six months for a tampon to degrade. Plastic packaging and applicators may persist indefinitely in the environment. Reusable sanitary protection, such as the Keeper, washable sanitary towels, and sponges are the best environmental option as there are no disposal issues to consider.

The percentage of waste paper pulp in tampons and towels has increased during the last ten years, but it has recently taken a dive again due to a move away from recycled products to a focus on premium ones. Manufacturers are playing to the fact that around half of women declare themselves prepared to pay more if they sense a higher quality and comfort level – hence the extra wings, gels and gauzy layers that keep appearing.

- Keeper
- Lotus Pads
- Luna Sponges
- Many Moons
- Natracare
- Soft-Tampons

- Bodyform
- Helen Harper
- Libresse
- Li-lets

- Alldays
- Always
- Carefree
- Kotex
- Tampax

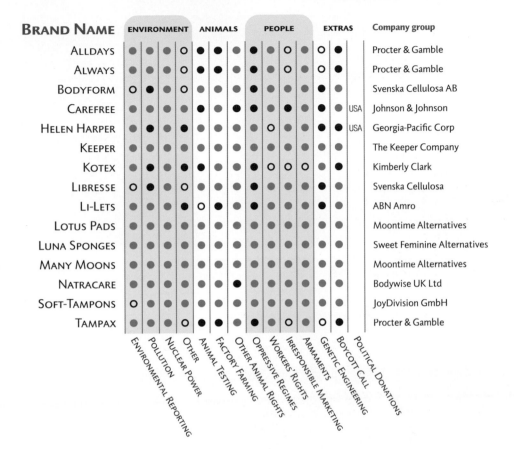

BRAND NAME	ENVIRONMENT	ANIMALS	PEOPLE	EXTRAS	Company group
ALLDAYS					Procter & Gamble
ALWAYS					Procter & Gamble
BODYFORM					Svenska Cellulosa AB
CAREFREE					Johnson & Johnson
HELEN HARPER					Georgia-Pacific Corp
KEEPER					The Keeper Company
KOTEX					Kimberly Clark
LIBRESSE					Svenska Cellulosa
LI-LETS					ABN Amro
LOTUS PADS					Moontime Alternatives
LUNA SPONGES					Sweet Feminine Alternatives
MANY MOONS					Moontime Alternatives
NATRACARE					Bodywise UK Ltd
SOFT-TAMPONS					JoyDivision GmbH
TAMPAX					Procter & Gamble

Column categories (diagonal labels):
ENVIRONMENTAL REPORTING, POLLUTION, NUCLEAR POWER, OTHER, ANIMAL TESTING, FACTORY FARMING, OTHER ANIMAL RIGHTS, OPPRESSIVE REGIMES, WORKERS' RIGHTS, IRRESPONSIBLE MARKETING, ARMAMENTS, GENETIC ENGINEERING, BOYCOTT CALL, POLITICAL DONATIONS

Key

● Top rating (no criticisms found)

O Middle rating

● Bottom rating

◉ A related company has a bottom rating and the
company itself has a middle rating

○ A related company has a middle rating

● A related company has a bottom rating

Source: ECRA-See page 14 for full key to symbols.

235

Sports shoes

Almost as soon as teenager shoe styles began to proliferate, the big sports shoe manufacturers came under increasing flak about the working practices in their factories in south east Asia and Latin America. This report looks at the major sports shoe brands (shoes used in sports rather than for fashion) that are available in the UK.

WAGES AND CONDITIONS

A UK-based campaign group, Labour Behind the Label, has been lobbying companies, including Adidas, Nike and Reebok, to pay a better wage to workers. Its research has shown that workers have often not been paid enough even to meet their basic needs. A US group, Global Exchange, estimated that it would take just three per cent of Nike's annual advertising budget to pay all its Indonesian workers a living wage.

Campaigners have been pushing for companies to adopt independently monitored codes of conduct, laying down standards they should meet in their foreign factories. In December 1999, ECRA researchers received codes from five companies. Marks were awarded for each code, using the eight criteria listed here:

- No use of forced labour
- Freedom of association (unions) and collective bargaining
- Payment of a living wage
- Working limit of 48 hours a week, with a maximum of 12 hours overtime
- Provision of adequate and safe working conditions
- Elimination of child labour (under 15 years old)
- No discrimination by race, sex etc.
- Independent monitoring of code implementation

CODES IN PRACTICE

In the survey, it was noted that all the companies referred to 'minimum' rather than 'living' wages and that none of the companies allowed independent monitoring.

Puma scored 13 out of 20. It covered most criteria, including child labour and freedom of association, but referred only to wages covering 'basic needs'.

Adidas scored 12 out of 20. It was similar to Puma, but allowed workers as young as 14 where 'national laws allow'.

Reebok scored 10 out of 20. It produced a book-length code but still allowed a working week of 60 hours or more 'in extraordinary business circumstances'.

Nike scored 9 out of 20. It had no policy on collective bargaining or discrimination but made a 'public commitment' to independent monitoring in the future.

The Pentland Group's code scored 8 out of 20. It constantly referred to 'prevailing practices' and said that its code was for 'management guidance' and was not part of an employee's contract of employment.

Of course, there are many other factors to consider including broad issues of animal welfare and the environment. This is why Ellese, Mitre and New Balance come out best overall.

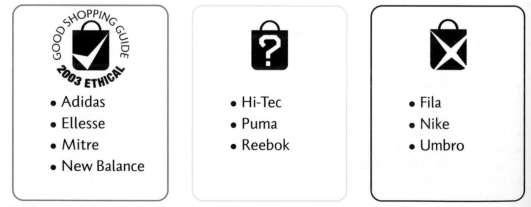

GOOD SHOPPING GUIDE 2003 ETHICAL

- Adidas
- Ellesse
- Mitre
- New Balance

- Hi-Tec
- Puma
- Reebok

- Fila
- Nike
- Umbro

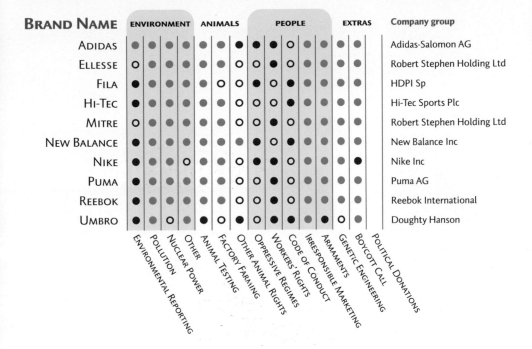

BRAND NAME	ENVIRONMENT				ANIMALS			PEOPLE					EXTRAS			Company group

Column headers (left to right): Environmental Reporting, Pollution, Nuclear Power, Other, Animal Testing, Factory Farming, Other Animal Rights, Oppressive Regimes, Workers' Rights, Code of Conduct, Irresponsible Marketing, Armaments, Genetic Engineering, Boycott Call, Political Donations

Brands and company groups:

- ADIDAS — Adidas-Salomon AG
- ELLESSE — Robert Stephen Holding Ltd
- FILA — HDPI Sp
- HI-TEC — Hi-Tec Sports Plc
- MITRE — Robert Stephen Holding Ltd
- NEW BALANCE — New Balance Inc
- NIKE — Nike Inc
- PUMA — Puma AG
- REEBOK — Reebok International
- UMBRO — Doughty Hanson

Key

- ● Top rating (no criticisms found)
- ○ Middle rating
- ● Bottom rating
- ◕ A related company has a bottom rating and the company itself has a middle rating
- ◌ A related company has a middle rating
- ● A related company has a bottom rating

Source: ECRA-See page 14 for full key to symbols.

YOU DON'T HAVE TO BE A
SPECIAL AGENT
TO PROTECT OUR FORESTS

Everyone can help. Look for the **FOREST STEWARDSHIP COUNCIL** label when you buy timber, garden furniture, flooring, paper, and other products made from wood. The **FSC** label is your assurance that forests are managed responsibly. That's why WWF, Friends of the Earth, Greenpeace, and The Woodland Trust all support the nonprofit FSC. For more information visit www.fsc-uk.demon.co.uk or call 01686 413916.

FSC® Trademark © 1996 Forest Stewardship Council A.C.

Pierce Brosnan photo donated by Nigel Parry, CPI

Nappies

Three billion disposable nappies are thrown away every year in the UK. As quick as spending a penny, or a pound, they're thrown in the bin and end up in our ever-expanding landfill sites. Disposable nappies contribute about four per cent to all landfilled domestic waste, at an estimated cost of disposal of £40 million. What a waste!

BUM FLUFF

The main disposable nappies arc Procter & Gamble's Pampers and Kimberly-Clark's Huggies.

The bulkiest component of disposable nappies (or diapers, as they are known in the US) is paper pulp fluff, for which the rising demand is beginning to threaten old-growth forests in Canada, Scandinavia and the Baltic states. Valuable wetlands, moors and meadows risk being destroyed in the quest for new plantations.

Other components include plastics and chemicals derived from non-renewable sources. There is controversy about the safety of some commonly-used chemicals such as the absorbing agent sodium polyacrylate. Babies with sensitive skin may react to absorbent gels.

HYGIENE

The average baby gets through about 5,000 nappies on its way to being potty trained. Disposables are commonly binned or, much worse, flushed away. Putting them in the bin without first cleaning off waste is unhygienic and, though few people know it, actually illegal. Chucking them down the toilet happens far too commonly, and they can cause serious maintenance problems in sewers and sewage farms. Many of them also end up in the sea – a Marine Conservation Society report found an average of between one and two washed up disposable nappies per kilometre of shoreline surveyed.

RE-USABLES

Re-usable 'terry' nappies really do offer a viable alternative to disposables. Only a small percentage of UK parents use them, but there is much higher use of re-useables in North America and Australia.

Terries used to be seen as hard work but washing machines have reduced this and there are plenty of nappy washing services available around the country, some run by local authorities. There are also plenty of new varieties, with specially fitted shapes and pin-free fastening systems, and re-usable overpants for added safety and comfort. The Real Nappy Association advocates the use of thin liners placed inside a terry, allowing solid waste to be peeled away and safely disposed of. These are biodegradable.

Real nappies help to counter nappy rash as they are breathable. But perhaps the best argument for them is the saving in cash terms – total nappy expenditure has been estimated at £250 for re-usables compared with as much as £700-£1,000 per baby for disposables.

- Svenska Own-Brands

- Pampers

- Huggies

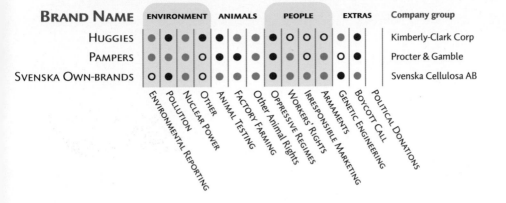

BRAND NAME	ENVIRONMENT	ANIMALS	PEOPLE	EXTRAS	Company group
HUGGIES					Kimberly-Clark Corp
PAMPERS					Procter & Gamble
SVENSKA OWN-BRANDS					Svenska Cellulosa AB

Column headers (left to right): ENVIRONMENTAL REPORTING, POLLUTION, NUCLEAR POWER, OTHER, ANIMAL TESTING, FACTORY FARMING, Other Animal Rights, Oppressive Regimes, WORKERS' RIGHTS, IRRESPONSIBLE MARKETING, ARMAMENTS, GENETIC ENGINEERING, BOYCOTT CALL, POLITICAL DONATIONS

Key

- ● Top rating (no criticisms found)
- ○ Middle rating
- ● Bottom rating
- ◉ A related company has a bottom rating and the company itself has a middle rating
- ○ A related company has a middle rating
- ● A related company has a bottom rating

Source: ECRA-See page 14 for full key to symbols.

Good Shopping

ECRA

The vast majority of the research featured in *The Good Shopping Guide* comes from ECRA, who are the undisputed leaders in their field. Their gold-standard research combined with a fierce independence add to their growing reputation.

WHAT IS ECRA?

The Ethical Consumer Research Association (ECRA) is the UK's only alternative consumer organisation looking at the social and environmental records of the companies behind the brand names. ECRA exists to promote:
- universal human rights
- environmental sustainability
- animal welfare...

...by providing information on consumer issues which empowers individuals and organisations to act ethically in the market place.

ECRA therefore
- produces a magazine *Ethical Consumer*,
- maintains a publicly accessible database of ethically-related corporate information - Corporate Critic,
- and conducts research for campaign groups and ethically minded organisations.

ECRA was founded in June 1987 and is a not-for-profit, voluntary organisation owned and managed by its staff as a workers' co-operative. Proud to have maintained its independence, ECRA is funded almost entirely by readers' subscriptions and by adverts from ethically-vetted companies.

WHY ETHICAL CONSUMERISM?

ECRA believes that the global economic system should be able to pursue ethical as well as financial goals - a belief which is gaining increasingly wider acceptance. In a world where people feel politically disempowered, and where governments are perceived as being less powerful than corporations, citizens are beginning to realise that their economic vote may have as much influence as their political vote. This is true both for individuals and for institutional purchasers and investors.

Ethical Consumerism is not a replacement for other forms of political action, but it is an important additional way for anyone to exert their influence. In 2001 'The ECRA Manifesto for Change' was published. It outlines policy recommendations for the UK Government in its second term of office. A copy of this article is available on their website at *www.ethicalconsumer.org/aboutec/manifesto.htm* or in issue 72 of *Ethical Consumer.*

What is *Ethical Consumer* magazine?

Ethical Consumer was launched in March 1989 and is the UK's leading alternative consumer magazine. Each issue contains four product reports, looking in depth at the ethical issues raised by campaigners. It also has news pages and features covering the latest ideas in the fields of ethical investment, organic food, consumer boycotts and corporate campaigning.

Product tables present a summary of the information held on ECRA's database (see below) and written details appear in separate 'Research Supplements' available from ECRA. Information is presented in a way that allows readers to make decisions based upon their own beliefs and priorities. There are more than 200 product reports in print covering everything from Petrol to Pickles...and a full list of reports appears on the website or is available free from ECRA's office.

Ethical Consumer magazine is available by subscription and costs £19.00 for six issues. They also sell individual back issues of the magazine, Research Supplements and campaign postcards to send to companies. Subscriptions and reports can be bought by post, by credit card over the phone, or from their website. Contact details appear below, or see the subscription advert on page 249.

What is Corporate Critic database?

For over a decade ECRA has been creating a database of information in the public domain on potentially unethical corporate behaviour. There are now around 50,000 abstracts on nearly 20,000 companies. The information sources are international, and include reference publications from campaign groups like Friends of the Earth, commercial directories on the defence and nuclear industries and public records on pollution prosecutions and emission levels. Increasingly, information is requested directly from companies on issues such as environmental reporting, animal testing policy and codes of conduct. In 2001 ECRA created a separate subsidiary company called ECIS to manage and develop the database and company rating side of its work.

Guest users can access an on-line version of this database free, to see the type of data held on specific companies. To access more detailed information, users need to pay and charges start at around £50 for pay as you go, or £420 a year for a years unlimited access. For more information see *www.ethicalconsumer.org/corp_critic.htm*

What other research does ECRA do?

For people or groups wanting more information about the ethical record of a particular company group, ECRA provides a research service and costs start at £35 per company. ECRA also conducts independent research into the comparative environmental impacts of different products, and has researched the Green Building Handbook Volumes I and II (E&FN Spon 1997/2000).

ECRA has also produced detailed research on ethical issues in specific industry sectors and markets for campaign groups such Friends of the Earth and Oxfam. ECRA provides consultancy

services for companies like the Co-
operative Bank which have programmes of
ethical policy development.

CONTACT ECRA:
ECRA Publishing Ltd
Unit 21, 41 Old Birley Street,
Manchester
M15 5RF

Tel: 0161 226 2929 (12noon-6pm)
Fax: 0161 226 6277
mail@ethicalconsumer.org
www.ethicalconsumer.org

Cited Organisations

86 Ltd is the media consultancy behind *The Good Shopping Guide*, responsible for public relations, digital strategy and advertising.

BUAV The British Union for the Abolition of Vivisection

ECRA The Ethical Consumer Research Association

EIRIS The Ethical Investment Research Service

The Ethical Marketing Group publishes *The Good Shopping Guide*. A group set up to bring high level media expertise to cause-related projects.

Fairtrade Foundation exists to ensure a better deal for marginalised and disadvantaged Third World producers.

FLO Fairtrade Labelling Organisations International

FOE Friends of the Earth is the largest network of environmental organisations, represented in 68 countries

GM Genetically manipulated (modified)

Labour Behind the Label is a UK network of organisations supporting garment workers' rights

National Food Alliance is now called Sustain and campaigns for 'better food and growing'

Naturewatch is an animal welfare campaigning organisation

Soil Association campaigns for organic food and growing and sustainable forestry

Sustain Previously called the National Food Alliance, it campaigns for better food and growing.

WHO The World Health Organisation